WorkThink™

to achieve excellent results

The Exemplary Worker Book Series

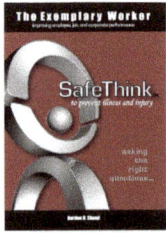

SafeThink™ ...to prevent illness and injury

SafeThink is a structured critical thinking strategy you can use to identify, predict, and control hazardous situations before, during, and after completing work. This cognitive-based safety strategy can be used on the fly, at work, at home, at play, and while driving. *SafeThink* also provides strategies for you to remain focused on your tasks.

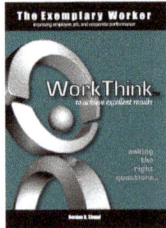

WorkThink™ ...to achieve excellent results

WorkThink is a thinking strategy you can use to achieve quality results with the least amount of effort. It usually takes little extra effort to do quality work instead of inferior work. *WorkThink* also emphasizes understanding the expectations of your supervisor, team leader, and customers so that you can achieve the excellent results they expect.

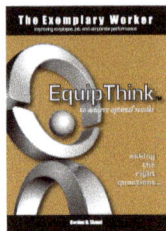

EquipThink™ ...to achieve optimal results

EquipThink is a thinking strategy for you to use tools, mobile equipment, and stationary equipment effectively and efficiently. The goals are for you to achieve the desired results with minimal stress on equipment, to conserve energy, and to extend equipment life. The input–process–output thinking strategy, in conjunction with identifying critical variables, is used to achieve optimal results.

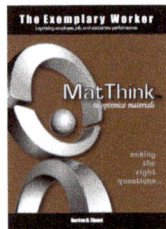

MatThink™ ...to optimize materials

MatThink is a thinking strategy you can use to make the most effective use of materials. The thinking strategy applies to recovering, processing, modifying, applying, transporting, and storing materials. Because equipment and materials are usually closely related, the input–process–output thinking strategy, in conjunction with identifying critical variables, is used to optimize material recovery and use.

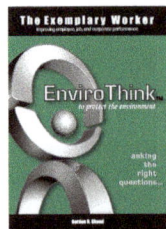

EnviroThink™ ...to protect the environment

Both industry and individuals have a responsibility to protect the environment. *EnviroThink* is a critical thinking strategy you can use to identify and respond to environmental issues for any job position that you might hold. *EnviroThink* helps you think through your work by asking yourself specific questions relating to environmental issues important to organizations.

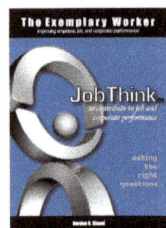

JobThink™ ...to contribute to job and corporate performance

Exemplary workers understand what is important to their organizations. They know the issues critical to business success and where to focus their efforts. *JobThink* addresses the critical thinking strategies you can use to identify what is important for job and corporate performance.

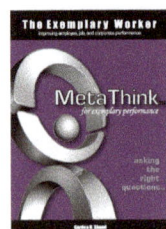

MetaThink™ ...for exemplary performance

MetaThink applies some of the thinking strategies addressed in previous books in different ways and also addresses new thinking strategies useful for the workplace. You can use these thinking strategies, along with the detailed thinking strategies addressed in other books of this series, to achieve exemplary performance.

The Exemplary Worker Book Series

"Rarely can workers from any sector access self-paced instructional materials that are easy-to-use, step-by-step guides to workplace learning. *The Exemplary Worker* book set is an exception. These books offer a good breadth of learning for workers in contexts ranging from: exemplary performance; job and corporate performance; results optimization; and work excellence. With meticulous organization, these essential training references are helpful guides for workers seeking to improve their performance. With prefaces designed to help trainers/instructors assist workplace learners, these books use critical thinking strategies that identify what matters to workers and supervisors considering people, equipment, materials, environments, and organization in concert."

—**Eugene G. Kowch, Ph.D.**, Leading Complex and Adaptive Learning
Systems/Organizations, University of Calgary, Canada

"The power of thinking in determining our safety, health, and welfare is obvious, but how to manage such cognition or self-talk for injury prevention, self-motivation, and self-improvement is not so obvious. Answers are provided in this action-focused series of self-help books on *The Exemplary Worker* by Gordon D. Shand. He offers much practical information for leadership, safety, and well-being. Each of these books provides critical and structured thinking strategies for optimizing performance on several fronts, from improving safety and productivity in the workplace to actively caring as a teacher, parent, or friend."

—**E. Scott Geller, Ph.D.**, author of The Psychology of Safety Handbook; Alumni Distinguished
Professor, Virginia Tech; Senior Partner, Safety Performance Solutions

"These are very practical books. I, myself, have been interested in the fundamental processes of human thinking. For creativity there is Lateral Thinking. For exploration there is the parallel thinking of the Six Thinking Hats. For perception there is the CoRT school programme. *The Exemplary Worker* series of books provide frameworks for focused thinking about specific situations. The frameworks guide the thinker to deal with the situation instead of messing about. That is why the books are so practical."

—**Dr. Edward de Bono**, Author of Lateral Thinking and
Six Thinking Hats and creator of CoRT

The Exemplary Worker Book Series

WorkThink™

to achieve excellent results

Gordon D. Shand

HDC Human Development Consultants Ltd.
PO Box 4710, Edmonton, AB, Canada T6E 5G5
www.hdc.ca
www.safethink.ca

Library and Archives Canada Cataloguing in Publication
Shand, Gordon D.
    WorkThink to achieve excellent results / Gordon D. Shand.
(The exemplary worker book series)
ISBN 978-1-55338-054-2
    1. Employees--Training of. 2. Critical thinking. 3. Employees.
4. Work. 5. Excellence. I. HDC Human Development Consultants
II. Title. III. Series: Exemplary worker
HF5549.5.T7S527 2014   658.3'1243   C2014-902762-6

Published by HDC Human Development Consultants Ltd.

Published in Canada

HDC *Human Development Consultants Ltd.*

Website: www.hdc.ca
E-mail: hdc@hdc.ca
Phone: (780) 463-3909

Acknowledgements

Developing *The Exemplary Worker* book series has been challenging and rewarding. I am certainly grateful for all the help I have received to produce quality products. Over one hundred people have contributed to the quality of the content and presentation.

Generally, I developed the first draft of the books working on evenings and weekends. I would blitz the first draft for a book—I produced the draft in a month to three months. During those times, my family's gracious support allowed me to concentrate on the task and to dialogue with them about the concepts. Once a first draft was produced, consultants in my firm carried out several edits as time allowed. HDC's Production Department developed illustrations and formats to produce a book ready for validation by industry. Because the people from industry volunteered their time and some validations were conducted in sequence, the validation process for each book took up to six months or more.

Many staff contributed to the development process. I would like to acknowledge those consultants who struggled to gather relevant content when working with customers—they gave cause to identify the thinking strategies used by exemplary workers and to develop the training for HDC consultants. Many thanks to the consultants who worked so diligently with me to produce the books. They were adamant in adhering to our standards for quality, even when I was burned out and wanted to put closure to a topic. Thanks to Janelle Beblow, Art Deane, Alice Graham, Jean MacGregor, and Bruno Schoenfelder for the wonderful edits and feedback. Thanks to Phil Jenkins, Kris Vasey, and Denise Hodgins for developing the illustrations, formatting the documents, and creating the book covers. Thanks to Maria Peck for coordinating the validations and field tests and proofing text. Their personal support, commitment to quality, and attention to detail are greatly appreciated.

I have been exceptionally fortunate to work with so many wonderful people from industry. They have been great mentors—they have made many contributions to my personal growth. A special thanks to nearly a hundred people who have volunteered their time to validate and field test the strategies.

Who is *The Exemplary Worker* series for?

The Exemplary Worker series benefits:

- **Individuals** who want to have outstanding performance

- **Apprentices and students** who want to work safely and effectively

- **Supervisors** who want staff to be more effective

- **Trainers** who want to contribute to improved corporate, job, and employee performance

- **Trades and technology instructors** who want their apprentices and students to work safely and effectively

- **Instructional designers** who want to ensure that training is relevant, useful, and practical

- **HR managers** who want to improve the development and retention of exemplary workers

- **Operations staff** who want to optimize production and minimize losses

Contents

WorkThink™

Table of Contents (continued)

Preface

In addition to being skilled, exemplary workers use a broad range of *critical thinking strategies* to maintain outstanding performance. Exemplary workers know what is important to their jobs and organizations—they put their efforts in the right places by doing the most important things, doing them effectively, and doing them efficiently. Because they know what is important to the job and the organization, they effectively coordinate their actions with others and make decisions in the best interest of their organizations. Knowledge and thinking skills empower workers to achieve exemplary performance, be flexible as workplaces continue to evolve, and provide leadership within the workplace.

Exemplary performance can have many benefits for you, the line worker, lead operator, foreman, or supervisor, including:
- increased job satisfaction
- being recognized by your peers and supervisors as an effective employee
- increased potential for keeping your job during slow economic times
- increased potential for receiving salary/wage increases or bonuses
- increased opportunity for new or different work assignments
- increased potential for promotion

Each of the seven books in *The Exemplary Worker* series focuses on one of five domains (**PEMEO**):
- **P**eople
- **E**quipment
- **M**aterials
- **E**nvironment

Loss and/or optimization (LO) are the main themes for the domains, creating the word **LO-PEMEO™**. LO-PEMEO stands for Loss and Optimization of People, Equipment, Materials, Environment, and Organization. As an example: **L**oss to **P**eople is illness and injury; **O**ptimizing **P**eoples' performance is working effectively and efficiently; **L**oss to **E**quipment is damage and shortened operating life; and **O**ptimizing **E**quipment is using equipment effectively and efficiently. The books place a strong emphasis on using **thinking strategies** and **asking quality questions**—the goals are to minimize losses and optimize performance of PEMEO.

The series of books addresses both loss and optimization of each domain. We recommend that you complete each of the first six books in the sequence. However, the books can be studied in any order without difficulty. The last book in the sequence, *MetaThink*, should be read last. *MetaThink* applies some of the thinking strategies addressed in previous books but in different ways and also addresses new thinking strategies useful for the workplace.

Introduction to *The Exemplary Worker* Series

Over the last twenty-five years, the process of discovering *what's important* for exemplary worker performance has gone full circle. The process began for me when I interviewed exemplary workers to identify relevant training content. My premise was that exemplary workers know what is important for people to do their jobs effectively. Over time, it became apparent to me that one of the reasons exemplary workers perform so well is that they use a set of generic thinking strategies. After starting a consulting firm to design and develop training, I developed a comprehensive internal training program for our consultants and technical writers who develop training programs. The training focused on using generic thinking strategies and critical questions to identify training content that helps workers perform effectively. With a lot of support, I have revised our consultant training program and made it available to the public for people to learn and refine their personal thinking strategies to be exemplary workers.

The Exemplary Worker books are presented as a series. The same concepts underlie all seven books. For example, a safety incident may cause harm to a person and result in other losses—work may be suspended, equipment and materials damaged, the environment harmed. The organization could also experience unpredicted costs and have its reputation harmed. This introduction provides a framework and the key concepts that apply to the series. The discovery process and happenstances that led to the development of *The Exemplary Worker* series are explained to provide a setting and context to give meaning to the underlying concepts.

The Discovery Process

For me, the real discovery process began in 1985 when I founded the consulting firm HDC Human Development Consultants Ltd. (HDC) to design and develop customized technical training programs. I believed that it was possible to develop quality training for any industry without having an in-depth understanding of the organization, its technology, or the tasks that its people perform. The premise was that a well-thought-out instructional design and development process combined with effective consulting skills would be sufficient.

As founder of the company, I felt that I was successful in providing leadership to identify training content important to my customers—customers often asked me to do additional work. If I could do the work well, then certainly others in the firm could as well and, for some deliverables, do better.

The Plan

The plan was that I would work with customers to develop the outline of the training program (curriculum) and identify critical content for the program. The training program would be documented in one of three ways:
● a list of specific courses
● a list of general training objectives
● a competency-based training profile

Competency-Based Training Profile

The following illustration is a *partial* example of a competency-based training profile. The profile is a visual presentation of the competencies (tasks and support knowledge) that specific work groups require to do their work safely and effectively.

ORIENTATION	Complete Company Orientation	Describe Roles and Responsibilities	Identify Local Structures and Facilities	Describe and Use Communication Systems	Identify Customers and their Expectations
SAFETY	Describe and Use Personal Safety Equipment	Review Safety Handbook	Complete First Aid Training	Decribe and Operate Personal Gas Monitors	Describe Codes of Practice
ENVIRONMENT	Describe Environmental Responsibilities	Describe and Store Hazardous Wastes	Describe and Monitor Gas Emissions	Take Waste Water Samples	Describe and Participate in Spill Response Exercises
GENERAL KNOWLEDGE AND SKILLS	Describe Flammable Gas Measurements	Use Portable Multi-Gas Monitor	Describe Reciprocating Compressors	Prepare Maintenance Requests	
ROUTINE TASKS	Carry out Routine Equipment Checks	Change Process Filters	Describe and Change Corrosion Coupons	Monitor and Adjust Inhibitor Injection	Perform Housekeeping
SITE-SPECIFIC KNOWLEDGE AND TASKS	Describe Remore Process	Start and Adjust Remore Process	Describe and Change Remore Output Parameters	Perform Emergency Shutdown of Remore Process	Shut down Remore Process for Maintenance

Critical content for each competency is a list of the key issues a buddy or supervisor would emphasize when coaching the trainee. The end product is a *scope document* listing the key issues and ensuring continuity between competencies—no overlaps or gaps in content. As an example of a scope document, here is a partial list of key issues for the competency *Purge Piping and Station Systems:*

- replacing one medium with another to prevent combustible or toxic condition
- important to prevent:
  - people being exposed to toxic gases
  - possibility of a fire
- piping should only be purged after system has been opened and exposed to a foreign substance
- stations purged in preparation for startup
- some stations have automatic purging for specific piping and equipment
- automatic purging sequence must be checked
- always purge in direction gas migrates (up or down)
- criteria for length of time to purge include volume, pressure, and amount of connected equipment

In a profiling workshop, I used a brainstorming technique with four to sixteen of the customer's employees to identify competencies and critical content. The workshops were mentally demanding. On the one hand, I was concerned that the scope of training and performance requirements be limited and only address competencies and content that were considered important to the workers, their supervisors, and the organization. On the other hand, I was concerned that critical issues affecting people and the business were not overlooked. During these workshop sessions, I was constantly searching for relevant, useful, and practical content. What do the workers do? Is there a special way of doing the task? How do they know they are doing a good job? What can go wrong? How can the equipment be damaged or its life shortened? What do you mean by product quality? What about safety and the environment? Does the organization have special policies and ways of doing business? What is important and to whom or what? What questions should I be asking the group? I did not have a clear set of criteria or a structured thinking process that I could use to provide leadership in identifying training content that was important to the worker and the supervisor.

Working with Subject Matter Experts (SMEs)

I certainly believed that asking quality questions was more important than providing content. Answers to the questions could be provided by the customer's experienced employees. The term *subject matter experts* (*SMEs*) is often used to refer to the organization's staff who provide content to training consultants and technical writers. Unfortunately, some SMEs, having in-depth knowledge of the tasks, technology, and the organization, had difficulties identifying content important for training. These SMEs expected consultants to provide leadership to identify relevant content. I soon discovered that my consultants often had difficulties in providing leadership to SMEs trying to identify content that was relevant, practical, and useful. When reviewing the first draft of training modules, information that would help trainees do their jobs more effectively, efficiently, and safely would often be missing. Nor would the supervisor's concerns always be addressed. Sometimes, information would be included that was of little value in helping workers do their jobs well and making decisions in the best interest of their organizations. When consultants asked me for direction as to the types of content that were relevant for training, I could not provide a comprehensive explanation. If the company was going to be successful in the future, I needed to find ways to define content that was relevant, practical, and useful—content that contributed to employee, job, and corporate performance.

Customer feedback gave me reason to believe that I was providing adequate leadership to identify relevant content; that I was asking quality questions. The truth of the matter was I did not have a formal list of types of question I should ask. In many ways, I was relying on intuition to ask the right questions. I needed to find a way to articulate a content gathering strategy that consultants could use with a variety of customers in different lines of business, different technologies, different hiring practices and performance expectations, and different ways of conducting business. I needed to find a way to identify the specific types of question consultants could ask SMEs to identify important training content—content that would help workers perform their jobs safely and effectively and contribute to meeting corporate objectives.

To help our training consultants and technical writers gain a better understanding of our customers, their businesses, goals, and concerns, I took consultants along to the competency-based profiling sessions. Listening to the group discussions and individual insights about the work and the business always provided learning beyond the information recorded in the program outline and scope document. This learning should be valuable when working with SMEs to identify detailed content for the training resources. Having this preliminary knowledge about the customer seemed to help some consultants be better at identifying relevant training content, but other consultants continued to struggle. I concluded that knowledge about the customer was valuable but didn't give consultants the strategies they needed to provide leadership when working with SMEs.

The Importance of Training Content Being Relevant to the Organization, Job, and Employees

Project reviews with customers were very useful for gaining ideas on how to improve services and products. Feedback from SMEs was that HDC consultants asked more questions than anyone they had ever worked with before. On the other hand, our consultants felt that they didn't ask enough questions because relevant information had been missed. The real issue was to ask fewer questions but more *quality* questions—questions that addressed issues that were important to employees, the job, and the organization. Certainly, customers strongly indicated that identifying relevant, useful, and practical content was the most important quality concern they had regarding the development of training resources. Customers also were adamant that consultants provide direction and leadership when working with SMEs to identify relevant content.

At the close of each project, I would ask the customer what additional training might be useful for consultants to help them be more effective at identifying relevant content. Suggestions included that consultants could increase their technical knowledge, or have a better understanding about safety management systems, environment management systems, or management styles. In response to suggestions, we began providing additional internal training using off-the-shelf technical training materials when possible. The additional training helped consultants to better understand what SMEs were telling them but only resulted in marginal improvements in consultants being able to provide leadership to identify relevant content. I concluded that the knowledge is useful but not sufficient in helping consultants (and workers) to identify issues important to employee, job, and corporate performance.

To compound the problem of identifying relevant content, expectations in industry were changing from developing entry level training (do as I tell and show you and don't ask why) to exemplary level training (maximizing productivity and making quality decisions) and every level between those two extremes. These changing expectations created difficulties in determining the content and amount of detail to include in training and keeping within training development budgets. Customers were upset if training materials included content they did not want and were not willing to pay for. Customers could also be disappointed if the training did not include content that they considered important. In many ways, the concerns consultants had in understanding the customer's expectations are the same concerns an employee new to a job would have.

When I had worked with exemplary workers, I discovered that one of their strategies was to confirm expectations. So we used the same strategy and built more confirmation checks into the development process to ensure the content was what customers wanted. Unfortunately, the confirmation checks were good at confirming that the documented content was what customers wanted but did not effectively address concerns about omissions of content important to customers (e.g., safety, equipment life).

Identifying Thinking Strategies Used by Exemplary Workers

Developing internal training for consultants to effectively identify relevant, useful, and practical content proved to be very difficult. Having consultants participate in the profiling sessions to learn about the customer, developing scope documents, providing technical and organization training, and building in confirmation checks had some value but weren't sufficient in helping them to provide leadership to identify relevant training content.

The instructional systems design models I was familiar with generally placed a strong emphasis on instructional development processes and only provided marginal direction and strategies on how to provide leadership to identify content that was important to customers. Certainly, the design of instruction and the nature of the content had an effect on each other. I suspected that there were instructional designs in which generic module structures and generic types of content would work for some types of technology and associated training outcomes. It would be several more years, after we had a large inventory of customized self-instructional modules, before we were able to develop a set of generic boilerplates (list of section and sub-section titles) for specific technologies and training outcomes. These *boilerplates* provided general structures for self-instruction and listed the types of content that *could* be included (but not necessarily included) in each section. No doubt, the SMEs that I worked with had mentally created their own boilerplates to be effective when working with specific types of equipment.

My initial effort to develop training to identify relevant content proved to be fairly impractical. Fortunately, several events provided me with the fundamental concepts needed to develop strategies that consultants could use to identify relevant content.

One of HDC's customers had a very demanding supervisor who was exceptionally analytical. In fact, he was by far the most powerful analytical thinker I have met. He was also driven to prevent anything negative from happening. He would always be analyzing situations and wanted to know all the *hows* and *whys* about every aspect of the instructional design that came to mind. Once a week I would make a personal visit to address his concerns. On one of those visits, he demanded to know what type of content should be addressed in the training. He said he asked our consultant the same question and the consultant's response was that *he would write self-instruction on anything as long as we told him the content.* Obviously, the consultant was not providing leadership when working with the SME to identify training content that would help the operators perform their work safely and effectively. For me, it was confirmation that our internal training was not very effective in helping our consultants to provide leadership.

My immediate response to his demand was to give some general criteria for identifying relevant content. *Well, safety, environment, equipment life, product quality, and customer satisfaction are important. Adhering to legislation and making decisions are important, too.*

There was a long silence—a lot of mental processing was going on in his head. Finally, he nodded and said, *Good. Let's tell the consultant and the senior operator what you just said.* The bottom line for this customer was that the training we were developing would contribute to his staff doing their work effectively and safely and making good decisions.

The interaction I had with that customer was the moment of discovery for me! The three-hour drive back to the office gave me time to reflect on what had just happened. Obviously, until I was asked, I had not been able to see the forest for the trees. Ask any business person what is important to their business success and he or she would give a list of areas of concern similar to the one I gave to my customer. No doubt the business person's list would be more extensive and include additional concerns affecting productivity and controlling losses—all businesses want to get the most out of their assets, including their people. Businesses prefer to have exemplary workers, workers that contribute to business success. Certainly, the training we develop for customers must help workers be effective in doing their jobs.

Creating the LO-PEMEO Model to Identify Relevant Training

I reflected on the thinking process I was using to identify relevant content when developing training profiles and scope documents. The questions that I had been asking myself during the sessions addressed the optimization and prevention of losses primarily to People, Equipment, Materials, Environment, and the Organization as a whole. Surely, the questions would take on meaning when the work environment was considered. And one way of assessing the work environment was to consider the conditions, actions, and events within the workplace that affect PEMEO.

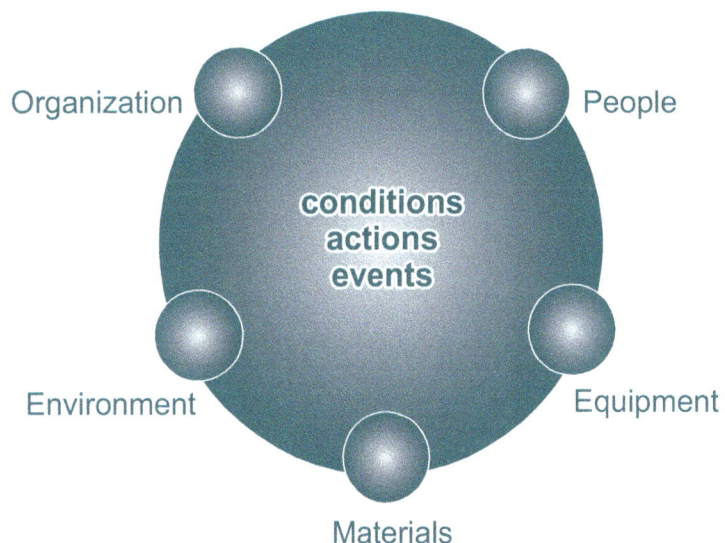

Most exciting for me, I could combine the concepts of optimization and controlling losses of organizational assets such as people and equipment to create a model and strategy for identifying relevant content. The LO-PEMEO model was born. Each of the five domains (people, equipment, materials, etc.) shown in the above illustration had potential for optimization and loss. An example of loss to people is illness and injury. Loss of materials when processing ore is the inefficient recovery of the desired products. Optimization of materials in construction is to use the right materials and maximize the use of the materials. The following illustration shows the combinations of loss and optimization of PEMEO.

LOSS				OPTIMIZATION	
Loss:	People	LP	P	OP	Optimization: People
Loss:	Equipment	LE	E	OE	Optimization: Equipment
Loss:	Materials	LM	M	OM	Optimization: Materials
Loss:	Environment	LE	E	OE	Optimization: Environment
Loss:	Organization	LO	O	OO	Optimization: Organization

Exemplary workers consider the potential for Loss and Optimization of each domain of PEMEO (i.e., LO-PEMEO) while they work. So LO-PEMEO was used as the framework and structure for *The Exemplary Worker* series of books. For example, loss to people (LP) is safety—the book *SafeThink* focuses on using a structured critical thinking strategy to identify and predict hazardous situations to prevent illness and injury.

Interestingly, several years later, I was introduced to a loss control model created by Frank E. Bird that used PEME as an acronym. I have always wondered if it would have saved me a lot of effort if I had known of Bird's loss control model earlier. Or would that knowledge have put in place constraints such that I would never have created the LO-PEMEO model?

While driving back to my office, I thought about how fortunate I had been over the years to work with a lot of exemplary performers, many of them my SMEs. Our customers gave us SMEs who are exemplary workers because the belief is that exemplary workers know what is important for business success and will provide training content that is relevant to corporate, job, and employee performance. When I had asked the SMEs if there were any concerns about issues such as safety, equipment, or materials, they would often look at the ceiling and ponder for a while. If they said yes, they would go on and give me further clarification. If they said no, I would continue to ask different questions. When I thought about it, the questions that I asked SMEs usually focused on concerns about LO-PEMEO. I always wondered what the SMEs were thinking when they were looking at the ceiling and pondering the answers to my questions. Eventually, I asked them. Interestingly, different SMEs from different companies and lines of business had similar concerns. For example, damage to equipment often involved shock from a sudden change in physical forces or temperature. The sources for causing damage could be people, material, or any of the other three domains. In fact, *each domain has the potential to affect the other domains.* Whether the SMEs were aware of it or not, they were mentally searching for specific workplace concerns relating to LO-PEMEO. In many ways, even at the detailed level, *the thinking strategies of exemplary workers were similar and generic.* Certainly, being aware of one's own thinking strategies contributes to planning and working effectively and helps to communicate effectively when collaborating with others and mentoring apprentices.

Linking Corporate, Job, and Employee Performance

When organizations develop standards, procedures, and training, they want to realize an improvement in corporate performance. Improving *corporate performance* is often achieved by either filling a gap in performance or by preparing the organization to move towards new goals. The following illustration lists some criteria that can be used to measure corporate performance.

PERFORMANCE REPORT

Customer Satisfaction	UP
Production	UP
Product Quality	UP
Equipment Run Time	UP
Equipment Damage	DOWN
Energy Consumption	DOWN
Material Waste	DOWN
Personal Injuries	DOWN
Maintenance Costs	DOWN
Environment Damage	DOWN
Rework Time	DOWN

At the operational or job level, the supervisor also has concerns about performance. Within his or her roles, responsibilities, and authority, the supervisor is expected to maximize productivity and minimize losses. Improved *job performance* contributes to improved corporate performance. The supervisor therefore represents the concerns and goals of the organization and must use specific resources and assets (including people) to effectively achieve the goals. The supervisor must also be able to motivate, coordinate, and assign staff to effectively carry out the work. Furthermore, worker performance affects job performance which, in turn, affects corporate performance.

Employee performance affects business results. Employees are expected to work effectively and efficiently and make good use of materials and technology. Expectations of performance are articulated to line employees both orally and in writing. In turn, employees have concerns about understanding the expectations and working safely, effectively, and efficiently to meet the expectations. The following illustration is of a person new to a job asking questions relating to corporate, job, and employee performance issues.

What's important to the business?

What does the team leader expect of me?

What am I supposed to do?

How am I supposed to do it?

How do I know I've done well?

How does my work affect others?

Is there a better way?

What tools and equipment are used?

Could I get hurt?

Could I injure others?

Could I damage the equipment?

Does this product affect the environment?

How much waste is acceptable?

How can I prevent...?

Will the customer be satisfied?

What should I do if ...?

What would happen if ...?

Do I have the authority to take action?

What action?

Whom should I inform?

What does ...?

How does ...?

What caused ...?

What is the reason?

What are the consequences for ...?

What questions should I be asking?

What answers do I need?

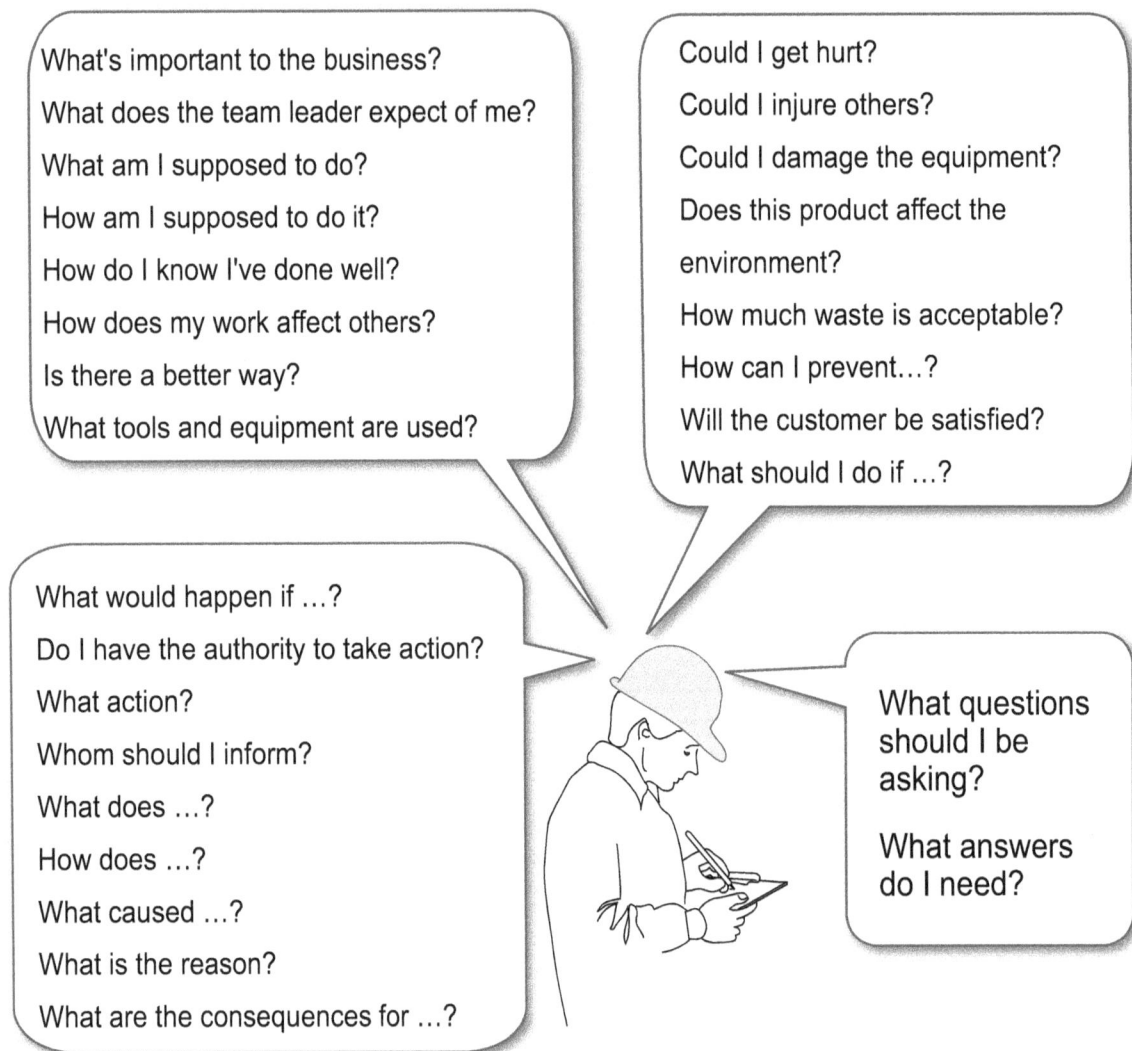

Many of the questions are generated by the LO-PEMEO strategy and focus on performance:

- What is important?
- What are the issues?
- What questions should I ask?

The person new to the job needs answers to the questions in the illustration to quickly learn to do that job effectively and efficiently. Interestingly, two employees with similar experiences and skills who are new to a job can perform quite differently. One employee will be uncertain about the work and become stressed if work conditions change. The other employee will initiate actions and make good work-related decisions for the organization within a few weeks. One of the factors that makes the difference in performance between the two employees is the knowledge about what is important to job and corporate performance. Understanding *what is important* provides criteria for focusing one's efforts and for making decisions. LO-PEMEO is a good start in identifying what is important to the organization. Although many of the issues identified by LO-PEMEO are generic, each organization has its own business strategies, resources, and priorities. As such, each organization could place a different emphasis on each issue identified by LO-PEMEO. And that's why asking the *right* questions is so valuable. Questions focus on key issues; the answers to the questions are unique to the organization, workplace, and specific circumstances. *The Exemplary Worker* series provides many of the questions that workers need to ask of themselves and of others to achieve exemplary performance.

Understanding Organizations for Exemplary Worker Performance

Exemplary workers understand what is important to the organization so that they put their efforts in the right places, do the right things, and make good decisions in the best interests of their organizations. For workers to have exemplary performance, they need to have an understanding of organizations in general, and a specific understanding of their own organization. Training and performance consultants also need to have a general understanding of organizations to be effective at developing customized training—training that is relevant, useful, practical, and reflects the organization for what it is. There is a lot of literature on organizations but most of it is more complex than training consultants need. Generally, the literature does not directly address issues important to designing and developing customized training for industry.

So, what issues are important? For consultants at HDC (and exemplary workers in other organizations) to be effective, they must be able to identify and understand organizational issues from different points of view. Imagine a roomful of statues facing in different directions. The room has many doors, each opened by a different work group or discipline. Each doorway has a different view of the statues.

For consultants to get a broader understanding of the organization, they need to view the statues from different doors. Ideally, consultants would walk around the statues to get many different points of view. The consultant must be prepared to consider different points of view within a specific organization to be effective at understanding the organization and identifying issues important to employee, job, and corporate performance.

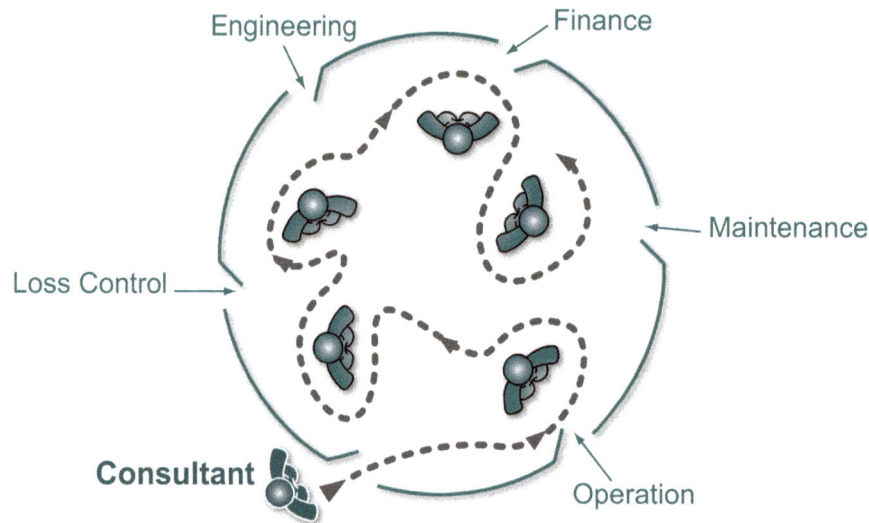

Both exemplary workers and training/performance consultants benefit from an understanding of relationships between business resources, organizational structure, business strategies, corporate objectives, and performance standards. Exemplary workers gain an understanding as to how their line of work fits into the organization as a whole. In doing so, they appreciate how their work affects others and they potentially make better use of organizational resources. This understanding about organizations also helps training consultants and technical writers to be more effective at designing and developing training that is customized, reflects the business, and has excellent value for the customer.

The approach I take with consultants to learn about organizations is to pretend to build a new business. Would the line of business be a service or a product? What is the mission? If the business is a service, then performing tasks is the main way to generate revenue and tools/equipment provide support for carrying out the work. If the line of business is to use technology to make products, then the technology dictates many of the tasks that workers must do. Having resources to achieve specific results is essential but not sufficient for business success. The resources must also be managed effectively. The following illustration identifies some key constituents of a business.

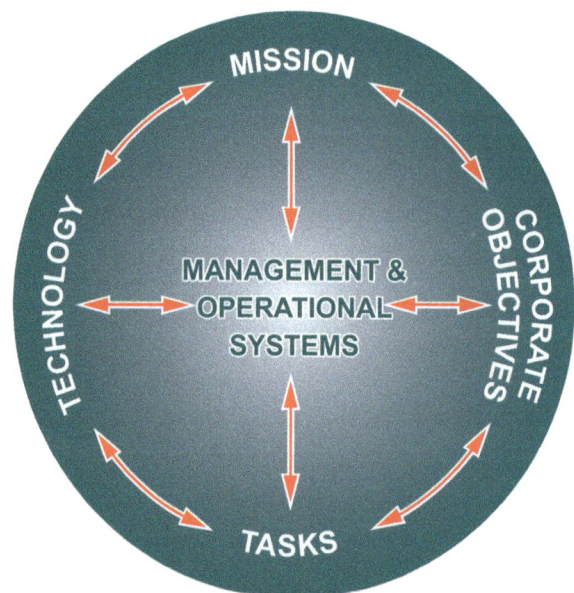

The book *JobThink* uses the previous model to provide a practical way for workers to understand organizations. This understanding helps workers to effectively focus their efforts and make decisions in the best interests of their organizations.

Of particular interest are the *corporate objectives*. Corporate objectives provide direction for using technology, performing tasks, and coordinating work to effectively achieve the corporate mission. The following table lists areas of concern, common to many organizations, for which corporate objectives may be developed.

Areas addressed by Corporate Objectives

- safety
- environment
- legislation
- equipment reliability and life
- equipment optimization
- energy use
- quality
- waste control
- loss control
- cost control
- customer satisfaction
- public image
- public disruption
- reputation
- communication
- teamwork

For a specific organization, a list of corporate objectives can be generated by expanding the organization's strategic business objectives or by using LO-PEMEO. Some companies issue strategic business objectives to provide direction to employees as to where to put their energy and focus for business success. Strategic business objectives identify what the organization must do well to be successful. For example, leaders in an organization may believe that it is essential for business success to have reliable service and satisfied customers. Organizations may identify five to eight strategic objectives. Within a department, the list of objectives (or goals) may be expanded in more detail to address issues specific to the department's mandate.

The expanded list of corporate objectives can also be generated using LO-PEMEO— each of the items in the above table relates to one or more of the LO-PEMEO domains.

Corporate objectives are fundamental to exemplary performance because they define what is *important* to the organization, the job, and workers. Corporate objectives provide a ***formal link*** between organizational goals and worker performance. Workers can use corporate objectives as criteria for working effectively and efficiently and for making decisions in the best interest of their organizations. Training consultants and technical writers can use corporate objectives to identify relevant, useful, and practical training content. Refer to my book, *Interviewing to Gather Relevant Content for Training* for:
- information about applying critical thinking skills to identify relevant content for training
- an interviewing process that consultants and technical writers can use to interview SMEs to gather relevant content

Developing Training to Identify What is Important to Employee, Job, and Corporate Performance

With the LO-PEMEO and business models, I could now develop training for consultants to provide leadership to identify relevant content. The LO-PEMEO model was the most practical approach to use to structure the training because it relates directly to work and job issues. The organizational model can be integrated into the training on loss and optimization of organization, LO-O. For the training on these models to be useful, the training needs to be flexible and apply to a broad range of work, technology, and organizations. The training must also provide strategies for people to think through their work. That is what exemplary workers do—they think through their work. And, the thinking processes are generic so they apply to all types of industries, work environments, and jobs.

All of the training to identify relevant content is founded on using thinking strategies. An emphasis is placed on *concepts* and *generalities* to maintain a broad application of the thinking strategies. Furthermore, the thinking involves asking questions relating to LO-PEMEO. Asking questions is important to maintaining the broad application of the thinking strategies and helping people remain mentally engaged. Asking the *right* questions is often more important than finding the answers, because if the right questions are asked, answers can usually be found— answers that contribute to exemplary employee, job, and corporate performance.

Over several years, I developed training for all the combinations of LO-PEMEO. I also expanded the training to include consulting processes and a performance and training model to design, develop, and implement competency-based training and performance management systems. I was very fortunate to have excellent support from staff to edit and refine the training. HDC staff made important contributions to the training content and presentation. And, after the training resources were in use, we refined them further.

Developing *The Exemplary Worker* Series

After the HDC consultants' training resources had been used for ten years, I decided to go full circle and modify the resources for general use. A major rewrite was required; the new audience was very broad and the lines of work very diverse. The instructional design content had to be deleted. New and different examples of applying the thinking strategies were required for the books. To help the reader, each book required new learning activities. Exemplary workers in industry needed to field test and validate the content. Staff also needed to make major contributions to ensure the quality of each book. It took over six thousand hours to develop *The Exemplary Worker* series. In addition, industry has volunteered more than a thousand hours to field test and validate the content.

The Exemplary Worker series has many suggestions to help you not only be aware of your own thinking strategies but also help you to refine your strategies to achieve exemplary performance. You will also be better at mentoring others to perform better.

Gordon D. Shand
Edmonton, Alberta
Canada

Training Objectives

Upon completion of this book, you will be able to:

- Clearly state expectations of performance for tasks that apply to your job:
  - what has to be done
  - how it has to be done
  - how well it has to be done
- Apply strategies to work effectively and efficiently
- Think ahead to plan work and predict consequences
- Identify communication and documentation requirements

Introduction

This book is one of *The Exemplary Worker* series of books. Books in the series all focus on using critical thinking strategies to identify ***what is important*** to employees, the job, and the organization. Each book focuses on one of five domains (**PEMEO**):

P People

E Equipment

M Materials

E Environment

O Organization

Within each book, loss and/or optimization (LO) are the main themes, hence the word LO-PEMEO™:

Themes	Books
L-P Loss to People (Safety)	*SafeThink* Use a structured thinking strategy to identify and predict hazardous situations.
O-P Optimize People's Performance	*WorkThink* Work effectively and efficiently.
LO-E Loss and Optimization of Equipment	*EquipThink* Use tools and equipment effectively and efficiently.
LO-M Loss and Optimization of Materials	*MatThink* Use materials effectively and efficiently.
LO-E Loss and Optimization of the Environment	*EnviroThink* Protect the environment.
LO-O Loss and Optimization of the Organization	*JobThink* Contribute to job and corporate performance.
LO-PEMEO Use thinking strategies for the workplace	*MetaThink* Integrate thinking strategies for exemplary performance.

The fundamental premise of LO-PEMEO is to *ask questions*. By asking yourself questions, you remain alert. By seeking answers, you continually learn and become more effective in the workplace and adaptable to changes. The big question is: *What questions should I ask?* The questions identified in LO-PEMEO help you to ask many of the right questions to do your job safely, effectively, and efficiently with minimal effort. Your goal is to meet or exceed your supervisor's expectations for doing the work.

Organizations hire people to do specific work and expect them to work in ways that contribute to the business goals. For most people, understanding and meeting work expectations is personally motivating. They tend to work towards meeting expectations because it increases their job satisfaction. Doing satisfactory work also increases the likelihood of being acknowledged for a job well done and receiving *good* performance reviews.

However, the ability to perform work effectively and efficiently varies from one person to the next. A person's ability to do the work to the organization's expectations is affected by a variety of factors, including:

- the person's ability to understand the expectations of the job
- the quality and suitability of tools, equipment, and materials
- the competence of the individual worker

One of the most important factors is a person's ability to understand the expectations for doing the work. Misunderstandings of work expectations can easily occur if:

- the work assignment is slightly different from previous work assignments
- the work assignment is new to the worker
- some pertinent information has not been communicated to the worker
- work expectations are poorly communicated and there is inadequate feedback to clarify and confirm the expectations

This book identifies the critical information that must be communicated and understood so that work can be carried out safely, effectively, and efficiently:

- *what* has to be done
- *how* it has to be done, and
- *how* well it has to be done

This book provides suggestions for working effectively and efficiently. This book also addresses the importance of thinking ahead to plan work and predict consequences. Communication and documentation requirements are briefly described. Throughout this book an emphasis is placed on the critical thinking required to perform the work satisfactorily. A set of critical thinking questions that workers must ask themselves is listed at the end of each major section. Workers need to ask these critical thinking questions to determine the most effective and efficient way of working to meet expectations. The concepts and examples in this book apply to many different industries, trades, and jobs.

The learning activities also help you to learn to apply the thinking strategy to your job and workplace. The Job Aid lists the critical thinking questions that must be considered to work effectively and efficiently—to do the right things and do them right with the least amount of effort.

This book is for those who receive work assignments, foremen, supervisors, and team leaders. This book provides practical suggestions for:
- working effectively, efficiently, and with the least amount of effort
- clearly communicating work expectations

An advanced book *JobThink* provides suggestions for focusing your efforts in ways that contribute to improved business performance (increased equipment reliability, reduced waste, increased customer satisfaction).

Scope of Work

Most jobs require workers to carry out a variety of work assignments. When starting a new job position, one of the first things you need to know is what work you have to do (i.e., the scope of work) so that you can focus your efforts on the *right things* to meet expectations. You also need to know what you cannot do so that you don't get injured and/or do other people's work assignments. Job descriptions and performance standards are two important sources of information to help you understand what work you have to do.

2.1 Scope of Work Definitions

Organizations often provide job descriptions to help people understand the work they are expected to do (and, in some cases, expected not to do). Unfortunately, from one organization to the next, job descriptions can vary in the type of information provided, the level of detail, and the use of terms. The following definitions are provided for clarity of terms used in this book. When possible, the terms have been listed from the most general to the most specific.

Discipline

A discipline is an area of specialization or study. The application of specialized skills and knowledge relates to a set of jobs or occupations. Examples of disciplines include instrument technicians, gas plant operators, and industrial hygienists.

Job (broad definition)

A job is what one does for a living. The term reflects the type of work one does and may be equivalent to one's occupation (e.g., electrician). The term *job* may be further defined to include the specific type of work or application of work. For example, an electrician may do only maintenance work or only new construction. A job consists of a set of duties; duties consist of a set of tasks.

Position

Many jobs in an organization have more than one position. For example, a gas plant operator's position may be inlet operator or plant 5 operator. A position exists even if it is not filled by someone; for example, an organization may advertise for a person to fill the position of site trainer.

Duties

A duty is a subdivision of a job. A job usually includes several duties which are the major function of the job. For example, a pipeline station operator's duties may include station operation, housekeeping, and minor maintenance. For a specific job, duties and responsibilities may be equivalent. A set of knowledge, skills, behaviors, and attitudes are required for an employee to successfully complete his/her duties. Each duty is made up of a set of tasks.

Tasks

A task is a work activity that is part of a duty. A task has several features:
• it can be assigned to one or more people to do
• it has a beginning and an end
• a person doing a task can usually be observed
• the result of performing a task can often be measured
  (e.g., in terms of quality, quantity, time, and timeliness)

Examples of tasks are collecting water samples, monitoring equipment condition, starting compressor #5, and removing old carpet from a house.

Job (narrow definition)

The term job is often used to mean a specific work assignment or unit of work. The job has a beginning and an end as in *When you have completed that job, come and see me.* An example of a job could be to install a new roof on a specific building. A job often requires several different tasks to be performed.

NOTE

The narrower definition of the term *job* is used in this book.

Lines of authority

Within a department, the immediate line of authority is the person to whom we normally report: the foreman, supervisor, team leader, or manager (i.e., the boss). That person delegates work and makes decisions in accordance with his or her limits of authority specified by the department. In large organizations, different departments have been given authority specific to that department's responsibilities. For specific issues, employees may have to communicate with departments other than their own, for example, with health and safety, environment, human resources, or accounting departments. Often, communication within and between departments is a critical issue that affects the efficiency and effectiveness of work.

Limits of authority

Within each job position, a person is given some degree of authority to make decisions and take action. The specific authority that one is given depends on a number of factors:
- The organizational structure that is in place can affect the scope or limits of authority for each job position. The organization may define the authority of each job position in general terms.
- The particular management style of the organization affects how decisions are made. For example, a self-directed team's decision-making process could require that all team members participate in the decision-making process rather than having one person make the decisions.

- The management style of the foreman, supervisor, team leader, or manager affects the type of decisions a worker can make. Some leaders are hands-on and want to be informed and involved in making many of the decisions; other leaders prefer to delegate as much decision-making as possible without causing undue risk of losses.
- The person making the decisions and taking action may have to have specific qualifications or certifications, for example, satisfactory completion of site-specific training, journeyman's ticket, certification by a professional association such as engineers and corrosion technologists.
- A person's competence and experience can also affect the degree of authority that is given. When people start in a new position, they may initially be given low risk, task-focused assignments. Over time, they may be given progressively more complex work assignments that require more difficult decisions to be made.

Job descriptions help people understand the work they are expected to do (and, in some cases, not to do). Written and unwritten expectations of performance further clarify the scope of work and work expectations.

2.2 Performance

The term *performance* can have different meanings depending on the level within the organization to which the term applies: corporate, department, job, or employee level. Performance can be defined as: doing something, activity, action, to carry out, execute, accomplish work, achieve objectives, achieve outcomes, achieve results. In this book, the term performance applies to employees and the expectations for carrying out *tasks*. Well-defined expectations of performance provide a benchmark or standard for assessing performance. In many cases, a person can be observed performing a task. Some tasks that require mental activities such as calculating cannot be easily observed. However, the results of the mental activities can be observed as proof of performance as well as for quality of the performance. Sections 3, 4, and 5 address information about tasks that is required to clearly define expectations of performance:

- *what* has to be done
- *how* it has to be done, and
- *how well* it has to be done.

What Has to Be Done

A critical part of understanding expectations is defining the task clearly. Understanding what has to be done is especially important when several tasks are similar but have a different application or result. There are several types of task descriptors that help define a task clearly so that you know specifically what you have to do.

Discipline: in some cases, worker qualifications or specialization must be stated because:

- only people with specific training and certification can do the work safely and effectively (e.g., electrician, pressure welder, second class steam engineer)
- some tasks are performed differently, depending on the specialization, for example:
  - perform routine compressor checks (*operator*)
  - perform routine compressor checks (*mechanic*)
  - check rectifiers (*operator*)
  - check rectifiers (*electrician*)

Action: tasks are stated using action verbs (such as *measure, mix,* or *start*) because people must *do* something (perform, take action) to achieve specific results. Verbs used to state a task must relate to a specific performance that can be observed (such as start, adjust, cut, clean) or a specific result.

Preconditions: sometimes certain circumstances require that the task be performed. For example:
- upon the *customer's request*, fill out the application for rebate form
- when the *bin empties to 25%*, fill the bin

Conditions: the conditions under which the task has to be performed can affect the way the task is performed and, in some cases, *how well* the task can be performed. Weather conditions, the operating effectiveness of equipment and technical systems, the type and quality of materials used for the task, and the application of the task affects *how* and *how well* a task is performed. Safety may be an important issue under specific conditions. Here are some examples of stating conditions for a task:
- pour cement if *the temperature is below 0° C (32° F.)*
- shut down the pump station under *normal operating conditions*
- apply a *lacquer finish* to the cabinet
- stack *K-2 blocks*
- dig house basements in *sandy soils*
- start compressor for *propane refrigeration system*
- locate pipe *buried in mineralized soil*

Materials: materials have been included in the above examples of conditions for tasks. For some types of work, for example, installation and repair, materials could be considered a separate descriptor for tasks. Different materials may require different tools and equipment and different procedures. Examples of material descriptors for tasks are:
- apply *rolled* roofing
- install *interlocking* shingles
- apply *two-component* epoxy paint

Tools and equipment: the type and size of tools and equipment and the type of stationary equipment that must be operated can affect the way a task is done, the safety of the worker, and the quality of results. Here are some examples of stating the equipment used to carry out a task:

- cut lumber to size *using a radial arm saw*
- cut lumber to size *using a chain saw*
- load fiber *using the F-105 loader*
- manually load fiber *using scoops*
- start *gas compressor #3*
- start *gas compressor #7*

Location: *where* the task is performed can sometimes be very important. If the task is performed at the wrong location, the work may have to be done again at the right location. In a specific workplace, the location may also imply conditions that affect the ease or difficulty of carrying out the task. Here are some examples of stating the location for carrying out a task:

- unload coal at *terminal 3*
- repair the inlet valve at the *Tamerack Station*
- perform a walkaround check of the *Nomac field separator*
- remove the old driveway at *85 Conner Rd.*

For a specific workplace, the location can affect the work and expectations for doing the task. As an example:

- Terminal 3 is very narrow, making it difficult to maneuver vehicles and equipment. It is very easy to damage adjacent property.
- The Tamerack Station is located in a low area and is always wet and muddy. Rubber boots must be worn when working at this station.
- A four-wheel-drive truck with a two-way radio is required to get to the Nomac field.
- Removing a driveway from the wrong house would be very costly.

If a person has to enter a confined space such as a trench, tank, or vessel, specific confined space entry procedures must be followed.

Note that, as a generality, the term *conditions* is often defined to include location, materials, and equipment.

Standards of performance: define *how well* the task has to be done. Sometimes standards have a major impact on *how* the work has to be done and *how long* it takes to complete the work. Take, for example, polishing stone to a low luster or a high luster. Changing a low luster finish to a high luster finish requires several applications of progressively finer polishing compounds.

Often, standards of performance can be expressed in terms of time, timeliness, quantity, and quality. For example:
- take orders from customers *within 2 minutes of their arrival*
- place all warehouse orders *before 10:00 a.m.*
- lay *7 pallets* of sod per day
- set mixers to produce *P24 blend*

Section 5—*How Well It Has to Be Done* gives a detailed explanation of standards of performance.

What is not.

Sometimes descriptors of performance indicate what *cannot* be used (e.g., tools) or be done to complete a task. For example, a house is being built and the yard has to be graded. The instructions are: *Grade the back yard at house #3. By the way, you cannot use the front-end loader because there is no access.* An experienced person who has been in this situation before while working for that particular company would understand how the work has to be done. Maybe! An important question to ask to clarify expectations would be, *What tools and equipment can I use to grade the back yard?* For further clarification, you could ask, *What tools and equipment can I not use?*

There are nine critical thinking questions you can ask yourself to determine the expectations for work.

Critical Thinking Questions
• Who does the work?
• What has to be done?
• What created the need to do the task?
• What conditions affect performing the task?
• What materials are required?
• What tools and equipment are needed?
• Where is the task being done?
• When must the task be done?
• How well must the task be done?

Learning Activities

The learning activities in this book can help you to be more effective at:
- understanding and communicating expectations
- identifying ways of doing work safely, effectively, and efficiently
- thinking ahead to plan and predict consequences
- identifying communication and documentation requirements

Throughout this book, an emphasis is placed on the critical thinking required to perform satisfactorily. The learning activities provide you with the opportunity to apply the thinking strategies to your job and workplace.

LEARNING ACTIVITY 1

What has to be done

Understanding the expectations when doing tasks is an important factor affecting your ability to work effectively. When you are given a work assignment, you need to ask yourself specific questions to ensure that you understand the expectations. If you have doubts about what is expected of you, ask for clarification. Learning Activity 1 helps you to clarify expectations about what has to be done.

1. List 8 tasks that you perform in your workplace. Your list of tasks will be used for other learning activities in this book. For each task, use the following table of descriptors to ensure that the tasks are stated clearly. For most tasks, not all of the descriptors are required to ensure that you clearly understand what has to be done. Refer to Section 5 for examples.

Task Descriptors	
• discipline • action • preconditions • conditions	• materials • tools and equipment • location • standards of performance

Task 1 _____

_____

_____

Task 2 _____

_____

_____

Task 3 _____

_____

_____

Task 4 _____

_____

_____

Task 5 _____

_____

_____

Task 6 _____

_____

_____

Task 7 _____

_____

_____

Task 8 _____

_____

_____

WorkThink™

Section 4

How It Has to Be Done

Often, there are several different ways or methods of performing a task. As part of understanding expectations of performance, you need to know whether you have to follow a specific procedure for doing a given task or whether you have the freedom to determine how you want to do the work.

Some tasks (critical tasks) must be performed in a specific way to ensure that:
- people do not get ill or injured
- equipment is used effectively and not damaged
- materials are used effectively with minimal waste
- work is performed efficiently with minimal effort
- the environment is protected
- quality standards are met
- total costs to do the work are controlled
- internal and external customers are satisfied
- regulatory requirements are met

NOTE Internal customers are co-workers, other work units, and departments within your company or organization. External customers are individuals and organizations that are not part of your company that use your company's services and products.

For critical tasks, an organization may have written procedures, practices, or guidelines. It is important to know the difference between these terms because they affect the way you can do the work. The definition of these terms can also vary from one organization to the next; one version of the definitions is provided below.

procedure: step-by-step actions to safely, effectively, and efficiently carry out a task to a specific standard. A procedure may also specify tools, equipment, components, safety requirements, and employee qualifications required to do the work.

practice: a practice specifies the way an organization does business. A practice can specify the requirements such as materials and equipment, employee qualifications, and general methodology that the organization expects to be used when carrying out specific work or responding to a specific issue. For example, it is HDC's practice that, when working on projects, the outcomes and deliverables are always identified and customer approval is given before work starts.

guideline: suggestions about the materials, equipment, and method for performing a specific work assignment or responding to a specific condition. The purpose of the guideline is to provide general direction to the employee. The employee has the latitude and flexibility to make changes in response to different work conditions.

code of practice: legislation and industrial associations require that organizations develop codes of practice for specific issues such as the removal and disposal of asbestos, entering a confined space, protecting the environment, and managing natural resources. Codes of practice include specific corporate policies that specify the way the organization does business to meet or exceed legislative and association requirements.

For many jobs, there may be very limited documentation on how to go about doing specific tasks. And, often, there is more than one way or method to perform a task. Each method may have advantages and disadvantages. You, however, are expected to do the task in a way that meets the expectations of peers, foremen, supervisors, team leaders, and customers. When there is more than one way of performing a task, you may have to decide on the *best* way to do the work. Here are some considerations to help you decide on which way to do a specific task.

1. Legislation and corporate policies may dictate how the work has to be done. For example, legislation requires that specific practices be followed for entering confined spaces. Legislation and corporate policies regarding heath, safety, and environment may dictate the use of personal protective equipment, the storage, transportation, and disposal of wastes, and the need for reporting and documenting events.

2. There may be a specific way of performing a task that is safer, takes less effort, minimizes waste and equipment damage, and gets better results than other ways. Specialists, such as trades people, often develop *tricks of the trade* to make work easier and get better results. For tasks that are considered critical, your organization may have written procedures. Procedures for critical tasks are often developed by a group of specialists such as engineers, and health, safety, environmental, operations, and maintenance personnel.

3. Sometimes conditions change, requiring modifications in the method for performing the task to ensure the safe, effective, and efficient execution of the task. For example, seasonal changes creating hot, cold, or wet conditions can affect the way a task is performed. The type or characteristic of materials (e.g., building materials, raw feedstock) can also affect the way the task is performed. In some cases the specific steps of the task can be adjusted to accommodate a change in conditions; in other cases, the method for doing the task has to be changed.

4. There may be a basic method and an advanced method for performing a task. The basic method may be very rigid, making it useful for training people new to a position. The advanced method may be useful because it

provides a more flexible and efficient way of meeting the task requirements. However, advanced methods often require that people have a significant amount of support knowledge or specialized skills to be able to apply the methods safely and effectively.

5. Sometimes two methods of doing a task are satisfactory but some people may prefer one method because that's what they are used to. On closer examination, however, each method may have different advantages and disadvantages regarding:
   - risk of becoming ill or injured
   - ease of doing the work
   - coordination or interference with other people and departments
   - control of quality
   - use of materials and amount of waste
   - effect on equipment condition and life
   - impact on the environment
   - total costs
   - customer satisfaction
   - meeting government regulations

WARNING

Often, people doing the work think of ways to make the work easier, more effective and efficient, and safer. However, care must be taken to ensure changes do not have a negative impact on equipment, technical systems, and work processes. Changes can sometimes be made to optimize a task to the detriment of other people and work processes. Optimizing a technical process without concern for the total operation can lead to unpredicted changes in equipment and process variables such as pressure and temperature. Equipment components may be subjected to excessive stress or be exposed to extreme environments that degrade components over time or cause immediate failure. Vendors, engineers, and loss control specialists may have to be consulted to ensure the changes will not cause losses.

---

6. Using different tools, equipment, and materials can make work easier and produce better results. However, costs

to do the work may also increase. Consideration must be given to determine if the benefits outweigh the costs.

7. Some people develop their *own special way* that is different from the way most others do the task. With practice these people have developed specific skills and muscles (especially for repetitive actions) to perform specific steps of the task efficiently and effectively.

8. A person's beliefs about what is important can also affect how he or she does the work and the quality of that person's performance. Here are some examples in the extreme:
    - get the work done in the shortest time possible. Safety and the quality of the work are less important.
    - ensure that each step of the procedure is performed to the highest level of quality possible. Time and cost to do the work are less important.
    - keep costs down by taking shortcuts, using materials sparingly, or using low grade materials. Product life, reliability, functionality, appearance, and safety are less important.

9. Some organizations have specific practices that must be applied to a group of tasks. For example, an organization could have a practice stating that all customers must be treated courteously. That organization may also specify ways of being courteous to customers when performing tasks.

Sometimes the sequence for doing specific steps of a task is important because of technical requirements and the need for safety, preventing damage to materials and equipment, or doing the work effectively and efficiently.

An important question to ask yourself, and perhaps others, is, *Why is this step or task done this way?* There may be good reasons for doing specific steps in a particular way or in a particular sequence. Understanding the reasons for doing work in a particular way is important for you to become efficient and effective at performing a task. Understanding reasons also helps you think through work more thoroughly when conditions change.

Section 6—*Work Effectively and Efficiently* provides additional information for understanding and meeting expectations.

NOTE

Many tasks can be performed by following step-by-step procedures. However, some tasks require the worker to have considerable knowledge to complete the task satisfactorily. For these types of task, it can be difficult to develop step-by-step procedures. A better approach is to develop a strategy for completing the task. For more information on developing strategies for tasks, refer to the Appendix 2—*Developing Practices and Strategies for Tasks.*

Critical Thinking Questions
• Is there more than one way of performing the task?
• Why would one method be better than others?
• Why is this step of the procedure done this way?
• Is there a risk of people getting ill or injured?
• Can tools, equipment, and materials get damaged?
• How much waste is acceptable?
• Can the environment be damaged?
• Is there a need for communication and coordination?
• Can the way the work is done affect costs?
• Can the way the work is done affect customer satisfaction (internal and external customers)?
• Is there an easier or better way of doing the work?

LEARNING ACTIVITY 2

How it has to be done

Understanding the expectations for how the task has to be done is an important factor affecting your ability to work effectively and efficiently. This learning activity helps you to clarify expectations about how a task is to be done.

1. From the list of tasks in Learning Activity 1, select a task for which there is more than one method for doing the work.

   Task _____

   _____

   _____

2. Write a brief description of two methods for doing the task.

   Method A _____

   _____

   _____

   Method B _____

   _____

   _____

   What are the major differences between the two ways of doing the task?

   _____

   _____

   _____

3. Most tasks consist of 2 to 5 major activities or steps.
   For example:
   - the major activities or steps for replacing a linoleum floor with new linoleum could be:
     − remove old linoleum
     − prepare the floor
     − install new linoleum
   - the major activities or steps to start a pipeline pump station could be:
     − carry out the pre-start checks
     − start the booster pumps
     − start the main pumps
     − increase throughput
     − monitor station operation

For the task you have selected, list the major steps in the proper sequence for each of the two methods.

Method A

Major Step 1 _____

Major Step 2 _____

Major Step 3 _____

Major Step 4 _____

Major Step 5 _____

Method B

Major Step 1 _____

Major Step 2 _____

Major Step 3 _____

Major Step 4 _____

Major Step 5 _____

4. This learning activity helps you determine which method is the best one to use. The following table lists a number of issues or factors, such as safety and quality, that are important to most jobs. Additional space has been given to add issues that are important to your job and organization. Using the table and rating scale, compare the advantages and disadvantages of each method for performing the task that you identified in 1. To complete this learning activity, think about the specific steps to complete each major step of the task. Ask yourself, *What are the issues associated with performing specific steps?* Place an N/A beside issues that do not apply to the task you have selected.

Rating Scale
4 excellent
3 good
2 fair
1 poor

Issue	Method A	Method B
safety		
protect the environment		
ease of work		
time to do the task		
damage to tools and equipment		
equipment reliability and life		
use of energy		
damage to materials		
waste of materials		
quality of work or results		
total costs to do the work		
coordination of work		
communication		
customer satisfaction		
adherence to policies		
compliance with regulations		

Using the completed table as a guide, select the method you think is the better method for doing the work. Note that you cannot add up the numbers in the columns because some issues are more important than others. For example, safety is more important than the time it takes to do the work.

5. Circumstances can change, requiring you to use a different method for doing a task. What changes in conditions, location, type or quality of materials, type of tools and equipment, or standards would make the second-best method a better way of doing the work?

    Method _____ would be the better method for doing the task under the following conditions:

    _____

    _____

    _____

How Well It Has to Be Done

For you to know that your performance is satisfactory, you need a means for measuring results. Standards define how well or to what degree of excellence the work has to be done and provide a means of assessing performance. Standards can apply to the results of performance for the task as a whole, major steps of a task, and specific steps. Standards can often be expressed in terms of time, timeliness, quantity, and quality.

time may be an important factor to achieve specific results and can also be used to measure efficiency of work. For example:
- all porous materials must be autoclaved for 10 minutes
- combine the two chemicals and stir for 3 minutes
- let the contact cement dry to the point where it does not stick to paper
- it should take a maximum of 6 hours to do this task

timeliness is about when some activity should start or be completed. Coordination and sequence of activities may also be important.
- you must arrive at work on time
- all lost-time injuries must be reported to the compensation board within 2 days of occurrence

- the area must be cleaned up immediately after the installation is complete
- starting at 2 a.m., the drying towers are manually switched every 4 hours
- the process must be shut down and isolated by 10:30 a.m. at which time maintenance work starts
- the materials must be delivered by 10:00 a.m

quantity can be measured in terms of amount and rate. For example:
- fill the bin ¾ full
- add 4 litres (1 gallon) of antifreeze
- set the delivery at 100 cubic metres/hour (630 barrels/hour)
- set the compressor speed to 480 rpm
- make 15 elbows/hour
- have zero customer complaints

quality is a complex concept that, for some types of work, can be difficult to describe. Often, quality involves the degree of precision, accuracy, or tolerance. Sometimes, quality standards for work include measurements of time, timeliness, and quantity (e.g., rates). Examples where measurement units are used to specify quality are:
- machine the parts to within ± 0.025 mm (1/1000 in.)
- set the product mix to 40% A and 60% B
- water content must be less than 0.5 %
- use an air hose that is rated for at least 500 kPa (80 psi)

The quality of a finished surface and fit of components can sometimes be difficult to describe. For example, a customer wants to order paint with a specific finish: *I want to buy a paint that is not flat but not too glossy either. And the texture must be smooth to the touch.* Seeing and touching the finished products is often the easiest way to understand the expectations for quality. A verbal explanation, pointing out the key standards for quality, could also help you understand the expectations for performance. For example:
- the finish on the table top must be smooth, have consistent color, and be free of scratches, bumps, and voids.
- the sheet metal parts must fit together firmly but not too tightly

- the guide must slide smoothly on the rail but not have any looseness

Often, several standards for quality must be used to describe the expectations of performance (see previous examples).

Knowing the standards for *how* and *how well* a task must be done can also provide you with the incentive for meeting the standards when doing the work. When people know the expectations for doing work, they tend to work towards achieving those expectations. There are many sources of standards, such as:

- ISO 9000 (quality)
- ISO 14000 (environment)
- legislated standards (boiler and pressure vessel, welding, electrical, hoisting, fire detection and suppression, occupational health and safety)
- standards associations
- professional associations
- engineering codes and standards
- manufacturer specifications
- customer standards
- corporate policies and practices
- performance appraisals
- peers, supervisors, and team leaders

Some tasks, such as *carry out pre-start checks* or *use a computer to monitor and control processes*, often do not have standards that are practical for determining if the tasks are performed satisfactorily. A person does these types of tasks satisfactorily by completing each step of the procedure correctly. The standard in these cases is to do the task in accordance with the steps of the procedure.

Using *indicators of performance* is a practical way of assessing performance, especially for tasks that have standards that are difficult to measure. Indicators are standards that indirectly represent the quality of performance. For example:

- A gas plant has four dryers to remove water vapor from the gas. One dryer is on stream, two dryers are in various stages of being regenerated, and one dryer is on standby. Every four hours, the dryers are manually switched so that a regenerated dryer is put on stream and the saturated dryer is taken off stream to be regenerated. Switching dryers requires a complex set of valves to be opened and closed. Both sequence and timing of valve operation are important to switch the dryers *smoothly*. After completing a dryer switch, operators go to the control room and check a chart on the wall (indirect indicator of performance). The dryer switch is done satisfactorily when the graph has a specific shape and all changes in the line are gently curved. Sharp and erratic changes in the graph indicate that the timing in the opening and closing of the valves was not done well. With feedback from the chart and practice, operators on all shifts achieve a satisfactory graph (i.e., satisfactory performance).

- Drivers of company trucks make deliveries within a 50 kilometer (30 mile) radius of the city. Driving a truck in a way that minimizes wear and tear is important. Keeping the truck clean is one indicator that the driver takes *good* care of the vehicle. A more reliable indicator would be maintenance records. Maintenance records for all vehicles are compared to determine a benchmark for satisfactory performance. Maintenance costs lower than the benchmark would indicate that the driver was driving the truck in a way that minimized wear and tear.

Indicators are standards that indirectly show whether or not the desired standard of performance is being met. Indicators are particularly useful when performing specific steps of a task. Ask yourself, *How do I know I have done this step satisfactorily?* and then identify the standard or indicator of good performance.

Indicators are also useful for quick and easy assessment of performance. However, for coaching and training, direct observation of the task being performed provides more opportunities to give immediate and precise feedback and encouragement about a person's performance.

Ease of doing work

Many jobs are easy to do; the hard part is learning to do the job.

Some organizations have written standards and procedures that apply to all shifts and locations. Refer to Appendix 1— *To Document or Not to Document Procedures* for a list of benefits of consistent performance standards and procedures. Appendix 1 also lists reasons for not writing procedures.

Critical Thinking Questions
• How well am I to do the task?
• How do I know that I have done the task satisfactorily?
• How do I know that I have done a major step satisfactorily?
• How do I know that I have completed this step satisfactorily?

LEARNING ACTIVITY 3

How well it has to be done

Understanding how well a task has to be done is an important factor for achieving satisfactory performance. This learning activity helps you to clarify the standards of performance that you must meet when performing tasks.

1. From the list of tasks in Learning Activity 1, select a task and state the standard(s) for satisfactory performance.

    Task _____

    _____

    Standard(s) of performance: _____

    _____

2. Using the task selected for 1, list the major steps and the standard(s) of performance for each major step. Your task may have less than five major steps.

    Major Step 1 _____

    Standard(s) of performance: _____

    _____

Major Step 2 _____

Standard(s) of performance: _____

_____

Major Step 3 _____

Standard(s) of performance: _____

_____

Major Step 4 _____

Standard(s) of performance: _____

_____

Major Step 5 _____

Standard(s) of performance: _____

_____

3. Using one of the major steps from 2, list three specific steps required to complete the major step and the standard(s) or indicators of performance for each step.

    Step _____

    Standard(s) of performance: _____

    _____

    Step _____

    Standard(s) of performance: _____

    _____

    Step _____

    Standard(s) of performance: _____

    _____

4. Review the tasks listed in Learning Activity 1. Select another three tasks and identify an indicator of performance for each task.

    Task _____

    _____

    Indicator of performance: _____

    _____

Task _____

_____

Indicator of performance: _____

_____

Task _____

_____

Indicator of performance: _____

_____

5. A test to ensure that you understand the performance
    expectations of a task is to ask someone else if he or
    she understands your explanation of the expectations.
    Write out a description of a task including: what has to
    be done, how it has to be done, and how well it has to be
    done. Give your description of the task to a person new
    to your job position and ask the person to:

    • explain in his or her own words what he or she thinks
      the performance expectations are. Note what he or she
      says about:
      – what has to be done
      – how it has to be done
      – how well it has to be done
    • state the degree of confidence he or she has about
      understanding the expectations for doing the task. If
      the degree is low, repeat the learning activity.

WorkThink™

36

Work Effectively and Efficiently

Understanding expectations of performance is a very important part of being able to do work satisfactorily:
- what to do
- how to do it
- how well to do it

Doing the work effectively and efficiently is an important part of achieving satisfactory performance. Working effectively means achieving the desired results or goals. Working efficiently means using the least amount of effort, energy, materials, and time to achieve the desired results. After many years of practice, a master craftsman does the work with ease and precision.

To efficiently achieve or exceed the desired standards, a number of issues must be considered:
- some organizations may not want the standards exceeded because it will cost more. For example, the desired properties of a metal alloy can be further improved by increasing the quantity of expensive rare elements present in the alloy. However, to use resources efficiently, the organization wants to use a specific amount of the rare elements to achieve the minimum acceptable standard for the alloy. In this case, the tasks that affect the composition

of the alloy must be done effectively to obtain production efficiency.

- some organizations are penalized if standards are not met. For example, in a gas plant, the agreement may be that the percentage of water in the gas stream is not to exceed 0.5% or a penalty will be levied. In this case, tasks associated with the composition of the gas stream must be carried out effectively to obtain production efficiency.
- for some organizations it may be costly to exceed standards but, when those standards are not met, the organization is penalized. The goal for these types of organization may be to exceed the standards by just enough to prevent producing substandard product should there be a change in operating conditions (e.g., electrical power or equipment failure, a rapid change in raw material composition). In this case, tasks affecting product composition must be performed very effectively and staff must be able to respond rapidly and effectively to abnormal conditions.

Ease of doing work

Being Efficient

One of the best ways to be efficient is to do the work right the first time.

In the above examples, working effectively contributes to the efficiency of the business. For many mental and physical tasks, the goal is to efficiently do the work to the desired standard (i.e., do the work in the minimal amount of time using the minimal amount of resources). For tasks where there is some flexibility in how the task can be done, the work can often be carried out in ways that makes work easier and more efficient, for example:

- using the right tools, equipment, and materials
- locating resources to complement the work
- sequencing procedures to minimize effort
- using *tricks of the trade* to carry out specific steps

Although many strategies to make work effective and efficient are specific to a technology or trade, there are some general strategies that apply to many types of tasks. Here are some suggestions:

- **gather** all the necessary tools, equipment, and components before starting the task

- **select** the right size and type of tools, equipment, components, and materials to make the work easier and more efficient. Making the *right choices* can minimize damage to the tools, equipment, and materials used to do the work, the equipment and facilities being worked on, and adjacent equipment. Two books in *The Exemplary Worker* series that can help you make the right choices are:
  - *EquipThink*
  - *MatThink*

- **locate** tools, equipment, consumable products, and materials in the *right* place to make the work easier, reduce unnecessary steps, and minimize the effect on other workers. For example:
  - Frequently used tools and equipment are placed close to the work but not so close that they interfere with the work.
  - Tools and equipment should not be placed where they can fall.
  - For actions that use both hands, parts, tools, and consumable products must be within reach.
  - In confined areas, materials such as piping, lumber, and flooring often have to be moved so that work can continue in that area. When possible, the materials should be moved to a partly finished area (not an unfinished area) so that the materials don't have to be relocated a second time.

WARNING

Do **not** place materials in a location that blocks an escape route.

- Large equipment and materials should be located in a place that does not restrict the movement of equipment and people.
- During work and after the work is complete, tools, materials, and documentation should be put back in their places, stored, or filed so that they can be easily located when needed.

- **sequence the tasks** to minimize setup time and waiting time. For example, work can sometimes be planned so that scaffolding does not have to be set up and taken down several times in the same location. Coordinating work so that people and equipment are not idle waiting for others to complete their tasks can make work more efficient and minimize costs.

- **sequence the steps of a task logically** so that each action leading to the next action contributes to increased efficiency and effectiveness. However, sometimes an extra step that does not logically lead to the next step is needed. For example, a part has to be located in a special place even though it will not be used until several steps later. This extra step is necessary because, when it is time to carry out the step requiring the part, there wouldn't be a large enough opening to pass the part through.

- **sequence the steps of a task** according to the physical arrangement of equipment and components to reduce effort and contribute to work efficiency. For example, in a process facility, it would be easy and seems logical to organize a list of equipment that must be monitored according to the process flows. However, at many facilities, the physical layout of the equipment and piping is not in a straight line. Equipment from one process may be mixed with equipment from other processes and between different plant floors. If the procedural steps for monitoring equipment were developed following the process flows, a person would have to continually walk long distances or go between floors. To make the monitoring task more efficient and less tiring, the equipment list could be sequenced so that all monitoring activities for an area or a floor would be done before moving to the next location.

- **reduce the number of repetitive actions** to accomplish the work to save a lot of time and effort. For example, a computer work document has 41 entries that are bolded, 40 of which have to be changed to plain text. Each of the 40 bold entries could be selected individually and changed to plain text. A more efficient approach would be to select all the text and change all 41 bolded entries at once and then rebold the one item that should have remained bolded.

- **get assistance** to handle and move awkward or heavy objects. Injuries and damage to materials, equipment, and facilities can occur when handling objects that cause excessive physical strain. Getting someone to help you or using moving equipment such as wheelers and carts can reduce physical strain and make the task easier and, in some cases, save time.

- **keep the work area clean** and organized. Some tasks create wastes such as scraps of material and dust. These wastes can get in the way of the work, potentially causing injury and making the work more difficult. Take the time to clean the work area and properly dispose of the waste. Put materials and tools that are no longer needed to one side, away from where the work is being done. Place materials that can be easily damaged in a location where they are less likely to get damaged (e.g., away from traffic areas). When the task is complete, clean up the area and put tools, equipment, materials, and documentation back where they belong. Good housekeeping makes the workplace safer and more efficient for everyone.

- **make use of the time** when there are delays, for example, waiting for a glue or grouting compound to set up. Work can often be planned such that, during the wait period, other steps of the task can be performed (e.g., clean up the area, take measurements, cut additional materials).

- **use *tricks of the trade* and *best practices*** for carrying out steps in a procedure. This can contribute to the ease and effectiveness of doing the step and reduce the number of steps to complete the task. Here are some examples:
  - Using an aid to carry out a step (e.g., using a sticky, non-contaminating substance to hold small roller bearings against a shaft while the shaft is being installed) can contribute to the easy completion of the step.
  - Carrying out a step of the task in a manner that reduces the number of steps required later in the procedure. As an example, when balancing equipment, a temporary counterweight is mounted on the rotating part. Mounting the temporary counterweight at the location where the permanent counterweight will be installed eliminates an extra step and avoids potential errors. If the permanent

counterweight is mounted in a different location from the temporary counterweight, the mass of the permanent counterweight has to be recalculated, reducing the efficiency of work and increasing the risk of an error.

– Making the best use of physical movements. For example, when working on a roof, always carry something (tools, supplies) when going up the ladder to save trips. Servers working in fast food restaurants can save a lot of steps by planning their movements.

– The method used to grasp and manipulate a tool can make the action easier, more effective, and less tiring.

– Cutting materials to size in a pattern that makes the most use of the materials reduces waste and costs.

– Using the right tools and equipment and using them with care can extend their life and reduce the risk of personal injury and damage to materials and facilities.

• **pace yourself** to minimize fatigue, especially for tasks that are mentally or physically demanding, require a high level of accuracy, or are boring. Working too fast or too slow can affect the efficiency and effectiveness of your work. Fatigue and boredom can reduce the efficiency and effectiveness of your work and increase the risk of injury. Work at a pace that you can sustain for a reasonable amount of time. Take short breaks during which time you can think about the next *chunk of work* (see Section 7— *Think Ahead*). To maintain motivation, set the next goal to be achieved before taking another break.

Critical Thinking Questions
• What is most important for quality?
• What tools, equipment, parts, and materials do I need?
• Is there a better way to make the work easier and save time?
• Can I get more use of materials and minimize waste?
• How can I prevent tools, equipment, and materials from getting damaged?

<table>
<tr><td>

LEARNING ACTIVITY **4**

</td></tr>
</table>

Work effectively and efficiently

Working both effectively and efficiently is important to achieving satisfactory performance. Of foremost importance is doing tasks right, that is, to the level of quality (standard) that is expected. Performing the task in a way that is efficient minimizes time, effort, use of materials, injuries, damage to tools and equipment, and costs. This learning activity helps you consider various strategies to work more effectively and efficiently.

1. From the list of tasks in Learning Activity 1, select a task and state:

   • what has to be done
   • how it has to be done
   • how well it has to be done

   Task _____

   _____

   What has to be done _____

   _____

   How it has to be done _____

   _____

   How well it has to be done _____

   _____

2. Using the task selected above, list the major steps. Your task may have less than five major steps.

   Major Step 1 _____
   Major Step 2 _____
   Major Step 3 _____
   Major Step 4 _____
   Major Step 5 _____

3. Keeping the major steps in mind, identify specific ways to perform the task effectively and efficiently.

Put your answers in the table that follows. Be specific; for example, in the *Gather* strategy, list the tools, equipment, and other resources. Place an N/A in categories where there is little opportunity to make gains in effectiveness or efficiency. A row at the bottom of the table has been left blank for listing a strategy that does not fit well in any of the listed categories.

Strategies to be Effective and Efficient	
Strategy	**Explanation**
Gather all tools, equipment, materials, and components before starting the task.	
Select the right size and type of tools, equipment, components, and materials.	
Locate tools, equipment, consumable products, and materials in the *right* place.	
Sequence tasks to minimize setup time and waiting time.	
Sequence the steps of the task logically.	
Sequence the steps of the task to reduce effort.	
Get assistance when handling awkward or heavy objects.	

(continued)

Strategies to be Effective and Efficient	
Strategy	**Explanation**
Keep the work area clean and organized.	
Make use of waiting time.	
Use *tricks of the trade* and best practices.	
Pace yourself.	

WorkThink™

Think Ahead

Think Ahead

One of the most important activities a person can do to be safe, effective, and efficient is to take the time to think through the work. Before performing a task or a major step, you need to take the time to plan the work and predict consequences (e.g., safety, damage to material, quality of results). Before carrying out specific steps of the task, you need to think ahead to be effective at achieving the desired results and preventing undesired consequences.

7.1 Plan Before Doing the Task

Often, careful planning before beginning work can contribute to improved safety, effectiveness, and efficiency of the work. The following planning strategy can be used for many tasks.

Work Planning Strategy

1. **Confirm the expectations of performance.**
   - what has to be done
   - how it has to be done
   - how well it has to be done

2. **Identify the major steps of the task.**

3. **For each major step of the task, consider the following issues:**
   - what has to be done
   - how it has to be done
   - how well it has to be done
   - the need to coordinate the work (who does what)
   - the tools, equipment, and materials that are needed
   - ways to do the work efficiently and effectively
   - potential safety hazards and controls to minimize illness and injury
   - impact on the environment and disposal of waste
   - likelihood of tools, equipment, materials, and facilities being damaged
   - cost-related issues
   - customer expectations
   - regulatory and industry requirements

4. **Carry out the pre-work preparation**
   - gather all the required resources including people, tools, equipment, components, materials, and reference documents
   - communicate with those who must coordinate with you to clarify the requirements to begin and complete the work
   - ensure the work area is safe to begin work

NOTE

Two HDC training resources provide strategies for identifying potential hazardous situations and using controls to minimize illness and injury before, during, and after a task is performed:

- *Analyze Critical Tasks*
- *SafeThink*

Companies often have written procedures and checklists for critical tasks. One type of checklist has one or two pages of introduction that address six to ten critical issues that affect performing the task safely, effectively, and efficiently. Issues that could be addressed in the introduction of the checklist are listed in the following box.

Issues that could be addressed in an introduction to a procedure
<ul><li>task name and application</li><li>standards of performance</li><li>purpose</li><li>worker qualifications</li><li>hazards</li><li>safety requirements (controls) before, during, and after the task has been completed</li><li>first response to potential safety incidents</li><li>worker response to abnormal equipment responses, conditions, and events</li><li>tools, equipment, and materials</li><li>quantity and specifications of parts</li><li>specific settings and tolerances</li><li>location of documentation</li><li>equipment and site preparation requirements for work to begin</li><li>coordination requirements with others before, during, and after the task is done</li><li>communication and documentation requirements</li></ul> **Note:** *Some of the above issues may be restated in the procedure.*

You can also use the previous list as another way of thinking about work and the preparation requirements for doing the task.

7.2 Plan Before Starting a Major Step

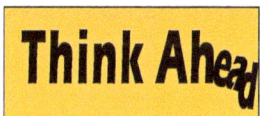

Think Ahead

One of the most important activities a person can do to be safe, effective, and efficient is to take the time to think through the work. One of the best times to think about the task at hand is after completing a major step. Often, people take a break before starting the next major step. During the rest period, issues about the next major step can be thought through and discussed with others in the work group. Refer

49

to Step 3 of Section 7.1—*Plan Before Doing a Task* for suggestions about issues that should be considered.

7.3 Think Before Taking Action

Think Ahead

Before performing each step of a procedure, you need to consider the positive or negative consequences that could occur as a result of:

- doing the step to the desired standards
- doing the step poorly
- having powered equipment not respond as expected

The type and severity of consequences also vary from one step to the next, from being insignificant to being very significant.

Doing the step to the desired standard

The expected results of performing each step are either clearly identified or implied. For example, the following statement specifies the desired standard, *Turn the temperature dial to 150 degrees Celsius*. The indicator that the step was successful could be a temperature reading on a gauge. Two questions you should ask yourself before performing a step are:

- *How well do I have to do this step?*
- *How do I know I have done the step well?*

Not doing the step to the desired standard

Steps that require a degree of mental or physical skill can often be performed with varied results. Three questions you should ask yourself are:

- *How do I prevent **not** doing this step well?*
- *How do I know I have **not** done this step well?*
- *If I do this step poorly, how do I correct it or minimize the consequences?*

Having powered equipment not respond as expected

Sometimes powered equipment can fail to respond to the operator's actions. For example, an electric motor may not start when the switch is turned on. Sometimes, if equipment does not function as expected, people can get injured, or equipment, materials, or facilities get damaged. Immediate action must be taken to prevent or minimize the consequences.

Before taking action to adjust equipment status or operation, ask yourself the following questions:

- *If I make an adjustment to the equipment, can I injure someone or affect other people's work?*
- *Could I damage the equipment, materials, or adjacent facilities?*
- *If the equipment does not respond as expected, can people, equipment, materials, facilities, or the environment be harmed?*
- *How do I know the equipment didn't respond as expected?*
- *What should I do if the equipment does not respond as expected?*

Assessing consequences before taking action

The consequences of performing each step of a procedure can have a positive or negative effect on People, Equipment, Materials, the Environment, and the Organization (PEMEO). To identify potential consequences, consider the Loss (L) or opportunity for Optimization (O) of PEMEO. The following table shows the 10 loss and optimization categories for LO-PEMEO.

LOSS				OPTIMIZATION	
Loss: People	LP	P	OP	Optimization: People
Loss: Equipment	LE	E	OE	Optimization: Equipment
Loss: Materials	LM	M	OM	Optimization: Materials
Loss: Environment	LE	E	OE	Optimization: Environment
Loss: Organization	LO	O	OO	Optimization: Organization

The following table provides some questions you can ask yourself to determine the consequences for each of the categories.

LO-PEMEO	
Category	**Questions you can ask yourself***
Loss to people (safety)	• *Can I get hurt?* • *Could I hurt others?*
Optimize people's performance	• *How can I do this step more easily? better? more effectively?*
Loss and optimization of equipment	• *How can I operate this equipment more efficiently and effectively?* • *Can I damage the equipment?*
Loss and optimization of materials	• *How can I make the most use of the materials and minimize waste?* • *What are the material specifications for manufacturing and processing?*
Loss and optimization of the natural environment	• *Can I damage the environment?* • *Can I enhance the environment?*
Loss and optimization of the organization	• *Will the customer be satisfied?* • *Can I reduce costs?* • *Am I following regulations?* • *Is there a requirement for coordination with others?*

*Additional questions could be asked for each category, depending on the specific task, application, and conditions. In addition to this book, other books in this series address specific LO-PEMEO categories.

For most steps, only a few categories apply. With experience in doing a task, you will be able to focus on specific categories that are appropriate for each step. The key issue is for you to think about consequences before taking action. And, if there are negative consequences or opportunities to be more effective and efficient, take action.

7.4 Think After the Task has been Completed

After a task has been completed, several issues need to be considered, including safety, consideration for others, communication, the environment, and equipment operation.

For example:
- Put away tools, materials, parts, and reference documents.
- Dispose of waste according to company policies.
- Clean the area. The area should look as good or better than when you started the task.
- Put up barriers and/or signs if there is danger that someone entering the area could get injured.
- Communicate with others who need to know that the task is complete.
- Complete, distribute, and file any required documentation.
- For equipment, start up cautiously and monitor equipment performance.

Critical Thinking Questions
• What tools, equipment, materials, and components are needed for the task?
• Do I have to coordinate or communicate with others before, during, or after the task is done?
• Could someone get ill or injured before, during, or after the task is done?
• What controls are needed to prevent injury?
• What is my first response if a person gets injured?
• How can I prevent tools, equipment, and materials from getting damaged?
• How can I operate the equipment more efficiently and effectively?
• How can I get the best use of materials?
• Could I damage materials?
• Could I damage the natural environment?
• How do I know a critical step is done correctly?
• What is the impact on PEMEO if a step is performed poorly?
• How do I prevent a step from being performed poorly?

(continued)

Critical Thinking Questions

- What should I do to correct the result of a poorly performed step?
- What should I do if equipment does not respond as expected?
- Are there any issues that could affect costs?
- Will the customer be satisfied?
- What has to be done after the task is completed to ensure the area is safe and tidy?
- What documentation is required after the task is done?

LEARNING ACTIVITY 5

Think Ahead

Think ahead

Thinking ahead before taking action is very important to achieving the desired results and preventing undesired consequences. This learning activity helps you refine your abilities to think ahead before doing a task, before doing a major step of a task, and before carrying out specific steps of a procedure.

1. A number of issues must be considered before starting a task. In Learning Activity 4, you considered issues to do a task effectively and efficiently. For this learning activity, use the same task you selected for Learning Activity 4 to identify issues affecting PEMEO. Keeping in mind the major steps for the task you selected, fill in the following table.

Thinking Ahead about the Task	
Issue	**Specific Concern**
Potential hazards before, during, and after the work is complete	
Controls to prevent illness and injury before, during, and after the work is complete	
First response to potential safety incidents	
Site preparations before work begins	
Most critical conditions, actions, or events that could damage equipment, materials, the environment, or organization	
Precautions to prevent damage to equipment, materials, the environment, or organization	
Most important issues for optimizing the use of materials and/or equipment	
Need for coordination and communication	

2. Select a major step of the task used for Learning Activity 5, Item 1. Think about what has to be done, how it has to be done, and how well it has to be done to complete the following table.

Major Step _____

Thinking Ahead about a Major Step	
Issue	**Specific Concern**
Need for coordination (who does what) and communication	
Tools, equipment, and materials needed	
Ways to do the work effectively and efficiently	
Potential safety issues and controls to prevent illness or injury	
Potential for tools, equipment, materials, or facility to get damaged and precautions	
Key cost-related issues	
Customer expectations (internal and external customers)	
Need for coordination and communication	

3. Critical steps are those which affect the performance expectations of the task or affect LO-PEMEO. Select a task from Learning Activity 1 that has critical steps. For each of the following learning activites, select a step that is appropriate for the activity and then answer the questions.

Task _____

_____

_____

Step that can affect the performance expectations for the task (result, outcome)

_____

_____

What are the consequences if the step is performed poorly?

_____

How do you know when the step is performed poorly?

_____

How can you prevent the step from being performed poorly?

_____

If the step is performed poorly, how do you correct it?

_____

Step for which equipment status changes or is adjusted

_____

What is the expected equipment response?

_____

How do you know the equipment responded correctly or incorrectly?

_____

If the equipment responded incorrectly, what is the potential negative impact on PEMEO?

_____

_____

_____

If the equipment responded incorrectly, what should be your first response to reduce any impact on PEMEO?

_____

_____

_____

Step that could affect the optimization (O) or loss (L) to PEMEO

_____

Identify the consequences (loss or optimization) for PEMEO of performing the step correctly and incorrectly. Note that some categories may not apply.

L-P _____

O-P _____

L-E (equipment) _____

O-E _____

L-M _____

O-M _____

L-E (environment) _____

O-E _____

L-O _____

O-O _____

How can you minimize or prevent negative consequences?

_____

_____

If there are negative consequences as a result of performing the step, what should be your first response to reduce the impact on PEMEO?

_____

_____

4. Select a task from Learning Activity 1. Use the following table to identify the actions to be taken after the task is complete. Note that some entries may not apply.

Task _____

Actions to be taken after a task is performed	
Issue	**Specific Concern**
Safety	
Put away materials, tools, equipment, components, and documents	
Dispose of hazardous materials and waste	
Clean up area	
Coordinate activities	
Communication	
Start equipment	
Documentation	

Communication and Documentation

Communication and documentation are critical to the effective and efficient operation of a department or business. Failure to communicate effectively can affect coordination of work and put people at risk of injury. Internal and external customers may be dissatisfied if communication and documentation are not completed promptly and properly.

8.1 Communication

At the job level, there are several reasons for communicating orally and/or in writing, including:
• clarifying and confirming expectations
• getting information
• coordinating work activities
• letting others know about pending actions or events
• informing others about conditions, actions, or events that have taken place

Clarifying and confirming expectations

When receiving instructions or directions, or getting agreement about a task that has to be performed, you must fully understand the expectations of performance. Ask yourself if you have adequate information about what has to be done, how it has to be done, and how well it has to be done to clearly understand the expectations of performance. If you have any doubts, ask specific questions to get clarification.

Sometimes you may think you understand the expectations of performance but you are wrong. One way to confirm your understanding of what is required is to explain your understanding back to the other person. You can introduce the feedback in several ways such as:

- *You're saying that...*
- *What needs to be done is...*
- *What I need to do is....*
- *What you want me to do is...*

Be specific in your feedback. Refer to Sections 3, 4, and 5 for specific issues that may have to be stated.

Getting information

Some types of information are important to know or understand because they can affect many aspects of the job (e.g., health, safety, the environment, equipment operation, and customer satisfaction). If you require information, ask someone or review the documentation. Some people are hesitant to ask questions. Considering the potential consequences of making uninformed decisions or taking the wrong actions, it is often better to ask questions before you start the work, not afterwards.

Coordinating work activities

Think Ahead

Some tasks require coordination with others in the work group, with other specialists, other departments, or with customers. Sometimes people become so focused on the task at hand that they forget about the need for coordination or the impact the task has on others. Think ahead. Ask yourself:

- *Who needs to be informed beforehand so the work goes smoothly?*
- *How do they need to be informed (e.g., in person, by phone, e-mail)?*
- *When do they need to be informed?*
- *What would be the consequences if they are not informed?*

Make sure that you notify others well in advance so that they have time to prepare and respond effectively. In some situations, letting people know at the last minute can be aggravating and can cause delays.

Letting others know about pending actions or events

Some tasks and specific actions can affect other people's safety or disrupt their work. Here are a few examples:

- remotely starting equipment that you cannot see. People working around equipment that is remotely started may be startled or injured. In process and manufacturing facilities, other upstream and downstream equipment and processes may also be affected when a piece of equipment is started, adjusted, or stopped.
- testing fixed protective systems such as fire alarms
- removing electrical lockouts and re-energizing equipment
- operating mobile equipment
- relocating materials
- erecting temporary structures

Inform others well in advance of pending actions and events so that they can adjust their work accordingly to minimize disruptions and prevent exposure to potential hazards.

Informing others about conditions, actions, or events that have taken place

Changes in the workplace can affect productivity and increase the risk of losses to PEMEO. Here are a few examples of changes that could affect PEMEO:

- the access door on a machine is cracked and could cause people to be cut when used
- the lift on a truck is temporarily out of order. Operating the lift could cause further damage.
- a vibration probe is temporarily replaced with another size. All readings of bearing vibration must be multiplied by 2 to get the correct reading.
- a stock of thick plastic used for decorative features is replaced with a softer plastic that scratches easily
- the company has banned the use of a specific type of solvent because it is environmentally hazardous
- the quality specifications for a product have been changed to meet customer requirements

Each workplace has its own protocols as to who should be informed when things go wrong. One of the most aggravating things for the person in charge is not being informed about an issue and finding out from a third party or a customer. The person you must inform about a problem may not be particularly pleased when told. However, that person may be even more upset by not being informed and *being the last one to know*.

Many methods can be used to inform others including:
- verbally, in person, or by phone
- memo
- posting warning signs
- keeping log books
- e-mail
- holding shift change and pre-job meetings

Communication about conditions, actions, and events commonly fails during shift changes and when people return to the worksite after an extended absence (e.g., after a vacation). Some companies have formal procedures for notifying people of recent changes; other companies do not. In either case, make it your responsibility to find out what changes have occurred.

8.2 Documentation

There are many reasons for documenting conditions, actions, and events in the workplace, including:
- tracking critical productivity and loss factors (e.g., process run time, quantity of production, waste, loss-time injuries, costs)
- tracking equipment condition and maintenance activities
- planning work (e.g., time, people, material, components, and equipment requirements)
- demonstrating due diligence (e.g., documenting when fire extinguishers are inspected and serviced)
- assessing project statistics to determine ways to be more efficient and effective
- completing timesheets and travel costs for invoicing purposes

For each task or work assignment, ask yourself key questions about the documentation requirements:

- *What has to be documented?*
- *How is the information documented?*
- *When should the documentation be completed?*
- *Who completes the documentation?*
- *Who receives the documentation?*
- *Does the documentation need to be checked or approved before it is distributed and filed?*
- *Where is the documentation filed?*
- *Is there a need to confirm that the documentation has been received?*
- *How does failing to accurately complete and distribute the documentation on time affect others?*

Critical Thinking Questions
- Is there a need to communicate before doing the work, while working, and after the work is complete?
- Who needs to be informed?
- When do they need to be informed?
- How should they be informed?
- Are there any documentation requirements?
- What has to be documented?
- When should the information be documented?
- How is the information documented?
- Does the documentation have to be checked and approved before distribution and filing?
- Who needs to receive the documentation?
- Is there a need to confirm that the documentation has been received?
- Where is the documentation filed?

Communication and documentation

Communication and documentation are important to the effective and efficient operation of a business. There are many different requirements for communication in the workplace. This learning activity helps you become more aware of the communication requirements of your job.

NOTE

A more advanced book *JobThink* addresses strategies that workers can use to focus their efforts in ways that contribute to improved job and corporate performance.

1. For each of the communication requirements listed in the **Purpose** column in the following table, identify a task that requires that specific type of communication. Specify the type of information that would be communicated and to whom the communication should be with. Specify any required documentation.

Communication and Documentation	
Purpose	**Task and Description**
Clarifying and confirming expectations	**Task:** **What** type of information: **Who** to communicate with: **When** to communicate: **How** to communicate:

(continued)

Communication and Documentation	
Purpose	**Task and Description**
Getting information	**Task:** **What** type of information: **Who** to communicate with: **When** to communicate: **How** to communicate:
Coordinating work activities	**Task:** **What** has to be coordinated: **Who** to coordinate with: **When** to communicate: **How** to communicate:
Letting others know about pending actions or events	**Task:** **What** action: **Who** has to be informed: **When** are they informed: **How** are they informed:
Informing others about conditions, actions, or events that have taken place	**Task:** **What** information: **Who** needs to know: **When** are they informed: **How** are they informed:

2. What communication and documentation would be required if a person is injured?

Who would be informed?

_____

How would that person be informed?

_____

When would that person be informed?

_____

What documentation would be required?

_____

To Document or Not to Document Procedures

Procedures That Need to Be Documented

Procedures should be documented when one or more of the following conditions exist:

- the employee does not have the specific skills and knowledge to carry out the task safely and effectively
- there is a need to document that employees can competently perform the task in a specific way and to an established standard (demonstrate competence)
- the organization wants the task performed in a specific way
- the task is complex
- the task applies to a specific equipment model or site-specific technology
- there is a risk of a negative impact on PEMEO
- there are optimization opportunities

To contribute to corporate performance, tasks must be performed in ways that align with and contribute to achieving corporate objectives/goals (e.g., maximize safety, adhere to legislation, maximize outputs, minimize waste, satisfy customers). While developing procedures, keep the corporate goals in mind and emphasize the goals when possible.

Procedures That Do Not Need to Be Documented

It may not be necessary to document procedures if employees who are given the expectations and reference information, such as equipment specifications, can do the job satisfactorily. For example:

- The task is simple such as parking vehicles and heavy equipment in a compound. In this example, the standards provide the criteria for parking (e.g., all vehicles and equipment have access to the gate, there is room to load and off-load other trucks, and there is easy access to heavy equipment for inspection and maintenance). If employees have the prerequisite skills to drive the vehicles and are given a plot plan showing the location and orientation of the vehicles, they are able to park the vehicles correctly.
- There is minimal risk to PEMEO if the employee makes a mistake. For example, the employee occasionally uses a basic photocopier or fax machine. If he or she needs assistance, someone could give a one-time demonstration.
- By way of the selection and promotion process, the employee has the skills and knowledge to do the job satisfactorily (e.g., journeyman tradesperson). For many tasks, skilled employees can do the work to the required standards if they are given the expectations and have access to the needed information.
- The employee provides assistance to another work group. For example, an operator assists maintenance personnel by operating the equipment and helping with the work. If procedures were developed for maintaining the equipment, there is a good possibility that the procedures were developed for the wrong audience and task (i.e., not aimed at operators).
- The task is performed infrequently. When the task must be carried out, the work is performed under close supervision of a competent person.

- The task requires coordination among several people, is potentially dangerous, or may have to be performed slightly differently from one application to the next. Tasks such as repairing the inside of process vessels and starting up a process after major modification may fall into this category. All personnel involved in the work have a pre-work meeting to develop a work plan and discuss safety. Policies and practices provide guidance for developing the work plan and may also dictate that employees have specific safety training before participating in the work.

NOTE

Companies in high-risk businesses often identify rate, and rank the risk of tasks that have the potential of causing injury or illness. For high-risk tasks, these companies may also carry out a critical task analysis to identify hazards and controls.

The following HDC training resources provide instructions, job aids, and checklists for conducting different types of task analyses:
- *Identify and Rate Critical Tasks—Relative Method*
- *Identify and Rate Critical Tasks—Quantitative Method*
- *Analyze Critical Tasks*
- *SafeThink*

WorkThink™

Developing Practices and Strategies for Tasks

Some tasks primarily involve the application of knowledge and require minimal physical activity. Quite often a paper-and-pencil test or observation of the quality of the results can be used to assess a person's ability to perform a knowledge task.

Often, knowledge tasks must be carried out under a variety of conditions. Issuing a Safe Work Permit is a good example. At times when a Safe Work Permit must be issued, operating conditions in the facility may vary depending on the availability of equipment, type of raw materials used, weather conditions, and throughput requirements. Maintenance work can create hazardous conditions and require coordination to ensure the work is carried out efficiently and safely. The combination of variables that must be considered when completing the permit makes it impractical to list all circumstances and document the required responses to each circumstance. Developing step-by-step procedures for some knowledge tasks such as completing a safe work permit is not practical either.

An alternative approach is to develop a practice or decision-making strategy for carrying out the task. To develop a practice, document only the major steps for carrying out the task. If there are a lot of decision points, developing a strategy which provides the decision-making criteria may be more useful.

NOTE Refer to the *JobThink* book for a comprehensive explanation of corporate objectives and their importance for decision-making.

The strategy can be depicted as an algorithm or flow diagram accompanied by an explanation of each decision point. One method to develop both practices and decision-making strategies follows:

1. State the desired result.
2. Identify and rank the general decision-making criteria. Often, corporate objectives or goals can be used as the criteria (e.g., safety of workers and the public, protection of the environment, protection of equipment, continuation of production, satisfaction of customers).
3. List the critical factors that impact LO-PEMEO (e.g., likelihood for toxic gases being present, need to maintain data communication, need to avoid false alarms, need to have equipment available to maintain production).
4. Group the critical factors (e.g., sources of energy that can harm people, factors impacting on production). Sometimes a critical factor is important enough or complex enough to stand alone as a decision point (e.g., enter a confined space).
5. Develop an algorithm or flow diagram that addresses the grouped factors. Each group of factors is presented as a question (e.g., *Are there any energy sources?*).
6. For each decision point on the diagram, develop a description and specify the required action. Use the general criteria developed in Step 2 to identify critical issues and determine the best course of action.

Refer to the following example of using a flow diagram to describe the decision-making strategy.

Safety Control Decision Chart

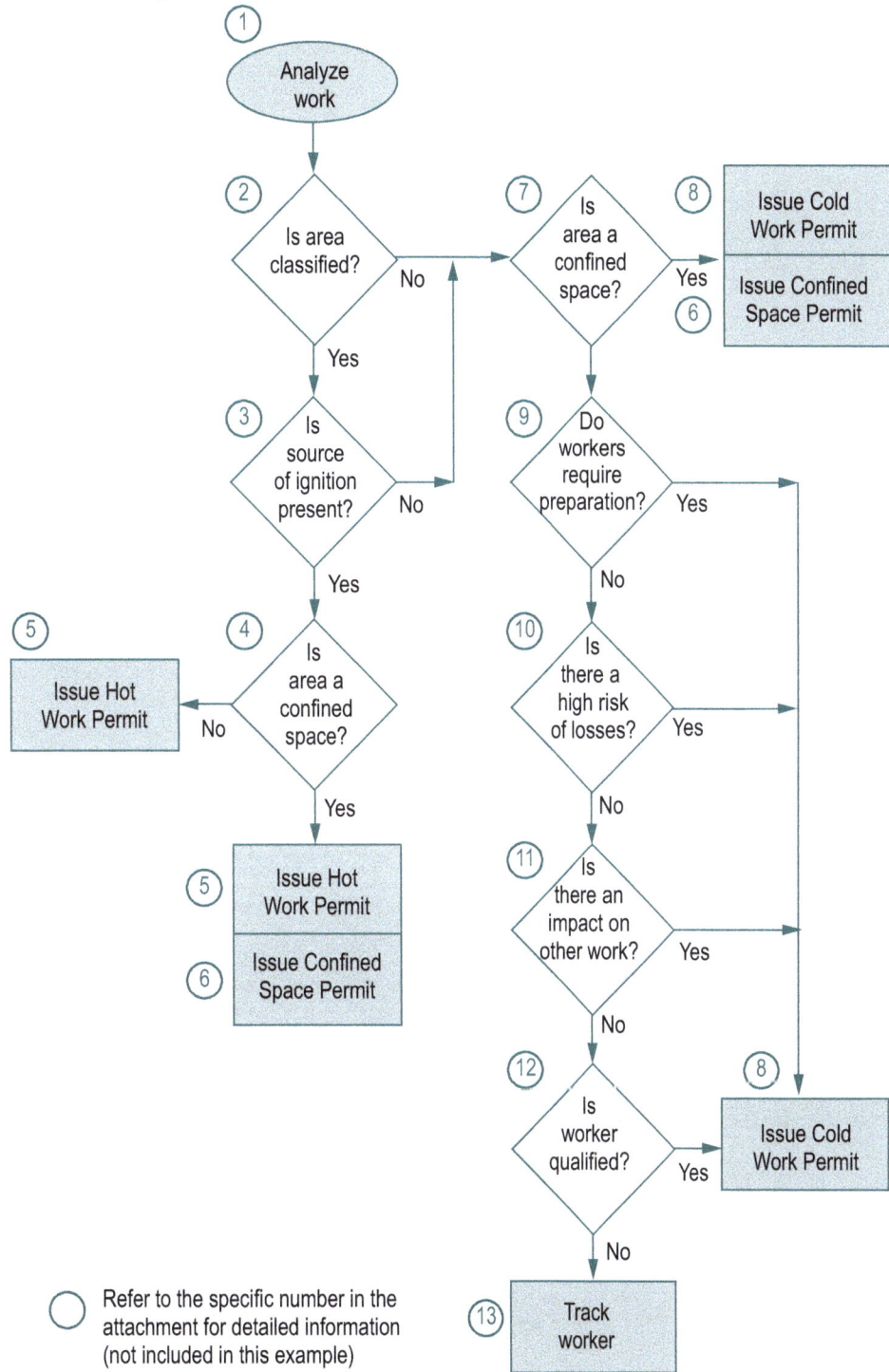

① Analyze work

② Is area classified?   No →
    Yes ↓

③ Is source of ignition present?   No →
    Yes ↓

⑤ Issue Hot Work Permit   No ←

④ Is area a confined space?
    Yes ↓

⑤ Issue Hot Work Permit
⑥ Issue Confined Space Permit

⑦ Is area a confined space?   Yes →
    ↓

⑧ Issue Cold Work Permit
⑥ Issue Confined Space Permit

⑨ Do workers require preparation?   Yes →
    No ↓

⑩ Is there a high risk of losses?   Yes →
    No ↓

⑪ Is there an impact on other work?   Yes →
    No ↓

⑫ Is worker qualified?   Yes →
    No ↓

⑧ Issue Cold Work Permit

⑬ Track worker

○ Refer to the specific number in the attachment for detailed information (not included in this example)

To use practices and strategies effectively, you must have prerequisite skills and knowledge. For example, to effectively issue a safe work permit, you have to be able to identify site-specific hazardous conditions, identify work activities that could affect PEMEO, use gas detectors, apply company policies, and adhere to legislation. Sometimes companies have a written policy stating the competencies or training an employee must have before doing a specific task. By identifying these prerequisite competencies you are either:

- ensuring yourself that you are competent at being able to carry out the strategy
- determining the training you require to learn to effectively carry out the strategy

Critical Thinking Questions

What Has to Be Done
• Who does the work?
• What has to be done?
• What created the need to do the task?
• What conditions affect performing the task?
• What materials are required?
• What tools and equipment are needed?
• Where is the task being done?
• When must the task be done?
• How well must the task be done?

How It Has to Be Done

- Is there more than one way of performing the task?
- Why would one method be better than others?
- Why is this step of the procedure done this way?
- Is there a risk of people getting ill or injured?
- Can tools, equipment, and materials get damaged?
- How much waste is acceptable?
- Can the environment be damaged?
- Is there a need for communication and coordination?
- Can the way the work is done affect costs?
- Can the way the work is done affect customer satisfaction (internal and external customers)?
- Is there an easier or better way of doing the work?

How Well It Has to Be Done

- How well am I to do the task?
- How do I know that I have done the task satisfactorily?
- How do I know that I have done a major step satisfactorily?
- How do I know that I have completed this step satisfactorily?

Work Effectively and Efficiently

- What is most important for quality?
- What tools, equipment, parts, and materials do I need?
- Is there a better way to make the work easier and save time?
- Can I get more use of materials and minimize waste?
- How can I prevent tools, equipment, and materials from getting damaged?

Think Ahead

- What tools, equipment, materials, and components are needed for the task?
- Do I have to coordinate or communicate with others before, during, or after the task is done?
- Could someone get ill or injured before, during, or after the task is done?
- What controls are needed to prevent injury?
- What is my first response if a person gets injured?
- How can I prevent tools, equipment, and materials from getting damaged?
- How can I operate the equipment more efficiently and effectively?
- How can I get the best use of materials?
- Could I damage materials?
- Could I damage the natural environment?
- How do I know a critical step is done correctly?
- What is the impact on PEMEO if a step is performed poorly?
- How do I prevent a step from being performed poorly?
- What should I do to correct the results of a poorly performed step?
- What should I do if equipment does not respond as expected?
- Are there any issues that could affect costs?
- Will the customer be satisfied?
- What has to be done after the task is completed to ensure the area is safe and tidy?
- What documentation is required after the task is done?

Communication and Documention
• Is there a need to communicate before doing the work, while working, and after the work is complete?
• Who needs to be informed?
• When do they need to be informed?
• How should they be informed?
• Are there any documentation requirements?
• What has to be documented?
• When should the information be documented?
• How is the information documented?
• Does the documentation have to be checked and approved before distribution and filing?
• Who needs to receive the documentation?
• Is there a need to confirm that the documentation has been received?
• Where is the documentation filed?

Another book by Gordon D. Shand

Interviewing to Gather Relevant Content for Training

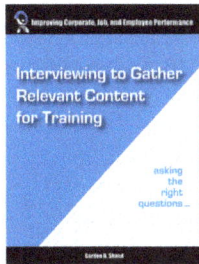

Effective training contributes to business success—**improved corporate, job, and employee performance**. But how do you figure out what training is effective? This book provides the strategies you need to identify training that will give you the best return on your investment in training.

Part A:

- provides criteria and strategies you can use to identify:
  - training content that is relevant
  - what content you should address and not address
- describes pitfalls that you can encounter and ways to resolve these pitfalls

Part B describes an interviewing process where you provide leadership to identify and gather content that is relevant, useful, and practical. You will learn how to:

- help the subject matter expert provide quality content
- select content that is relevant and eliminate content that will not improve performance
- keep the subject matter expert engaged
- structure the content to effectively and efficiently develop training and assessment resources

The suggestions in this book are the accumulated experiences of many training and performance consultants who have encountered the challenges of gathering relevant content and developing effective training.

Who can benefit?

- educational, training, and performance consultants
- training program designers
- instructional designers
- technical writers
- trainers and coaches
- internal staff who develop training